Spiritual Pregnancy

DISCOVERING YOUR PURPOSE

Kenneth W. Antoine

KESZA Publishing LLC
P.O. Box 1295
Marrero, La. 70073

504-994-6222
ISBN: 978-0-9963430-0-8 Paper back
Library of congress control number 2012901765
for more materials log on to:
www.store.kwaministries.com

CONTENTS

Acknowledgments

To my wife, Ethel C. Antoine, and my son, Seth: you guys are in a class by yourselves, and I love you for all your support and encouragement.

I would like to thank God for my mother and father, who are with Him right now, and for everything they did to make me the man I am today. They were a godly example for me. To my sisters and brothers: thanks for being there whenever I needed you. To my family members, natural and spiritual: thanks for everything.

To my church family, Royal Palace Ministries: I thank God for all of you.

INTRODUCTION

Often in our lives there are things happening in our heart that we cannot explain. We know that we are not losing our mind, but thoughts of something greater than we are keep us on edge. Here's what the Bible says:

> **We are assured and know that [*God being a partner in their labor*] all things work together and are [*fitting into a plan*] for good to and for those who love God and are called according to [*His*] design and purpose.**
>
> **For those whom He foreknew [*of whom He was aware and loved beforehand*], He also destined from the beginning [*foreordaining them*] to be molded into the image of His Son [*and share inwardly His likeness*], that He might become the firstborn among many brethren.**
>
> **And those whom He thus foreordained, He also called; and those whom He called, He also justified (acquitted, made righteous, putting them into right standing with Himself). And those whom He justified, He also glorified [*raising them to a heavenly dignity and condition or state of being*].**
>
> **Rom. 8:28-30 (Amplified Bible)**

Here Paul explains to the church that it doesn't matter what happens in life; God is orchestrating his master plan in our lives—and it is this plan that makes us wonder what is going on in our hearts.

If you are born again but feel as if there is something more you should be doing, you are spiritually pregnant. That's right—you're pregnant with purpose. God has a purpose for your life, and it is your job to find out what that purpose is. All the things you've been going through—the emotions, feelings, hurts, problems, and pains—are part of His divine will for your life.

It is my prayer that this book will give you insight into the process that we all have to go through to fulfill our divine purpose in life.

Chapter One

CONCEPTION

In order for there to be a pregnancy, there must be an egg and a seed. When the two come together, life is created. The egg must be receptive to the seed in order for the pregnancy to take place. The Bible tells us that a man and a woman must be married first, and then there can be intimacy. This coming together is for procreation. It is God's desire that a husband and wife be fruitful and multiply. The following scriptures show us that God has given us this power:

> God said, Let Us [*Father, Son, and Holy Spirit*] make mankind in Our image, after Our likeness, and let them have complete authority over the fish of the sea, the birds of the air, the [*tame*] beasts, and over all of the earth, and over everything that creeps upon the earth. So God created man in His own image, in the image and likeness of God He created him; male and female He created them. And God blessed them and said to them, Be fruitful, multiply, and fill the earth, and subdue it [*using all its vast resources in the service of God and man*]; and have dominion over the fish of the sea, the birds of the air, and over every living creature that moves upon the earth.

Gen. 1:26-28 (The Amplified Bible)

We can see here that God ordained that man and woman come together as husband and wife. When He created Adam, He gave him Eve, a wife suitable for him, that they should replenish the earth. It is God's design that man and woman should become one.

Once a marriage has taken place, God will bless the union with children. He allows the woman to conceive,

3

bringing forth the fruits of that union. The same thing must take place in the spiritual sense; we must marry God before He can bless our union.

Note that in Genesis 1:26, God says, "Let *Us* make mankind..." He is talking to Jesus and the Holy Spirit about His intention to create humans in His image. But God does not have a human body; He is talking about a spiritual being.

The word *image* means a likeness, imitation, representation, or similitude of something. The word involves the two ideas of *representation* and *manifestation*.

We can see in John 4:24 that God is a spirit:

> God is a Spirit (a spiritual Being) and those who worship Him must worship Him in spirit and in truth (reality).

John 4:24 (The Amplified Bible)

UNDERSTANDING THE THREEFOLD NATURE OF MAN

You are more than just a human being; you are also a spiritual being. In order for you to fully understand the concept of spiritual pregnancy, you must understand that there is more to you than just a human body: you are body, soul, and spirit. Remember, we are made in God's image and likeness.

God is a triune God. The doctrine of the Trinity means that within the being and activity of God, there are three distinct persons: God the Father, God the Son, and God the Holy Spirit. Although the word *Trinity* doesn't appear in the Bible, the Trinitarian formula is mentioned in 2 Corinthians 2:13:

> **The grace (favor and spiritual blessing) of the Lord Jesus Christ and the love of God and the presence and fellowship (the communion and sharing together, and participation) in the Holy Spirit be with you all. Amen (so be it).**

Just as it states in Genesis, God created the world, but He was not alone. The Bible says that as He spoke, the Spirit moved:

> **The earth was without form and an empty waste, and darkness was upon the face of the very great deep. The Spirit of God was moving (hovering, brooding) over the face of the waters.**
>
> **Gen. 1:2 (The Amplified Bible)**

Note that in the following verses from Genesis, God is now talking to the man and woman:

> **And God blessed them and said to them, Be fruitful, multiply, and fill the earth, and subdue it [*using all its vast resources in the service of God and man*]; and have dominion over the fish of the sea, the birds of the air, and over every living creature that moves upon the earth. And God said, See, I have given you every plant yielding seed that is on the face of all the land and every tree with seed in its fruit; you shall have them for food.**
>
> Gen. 1:28-29 **(The Amplified Bible)**

God tells man and woman to be fruitful and multiply; He also tells them to see what He has given them. This is extremely important, because he has not yet created their human bodies. Let's now look at Genesis 2:7, in which He creates their bodies:

Then the Lord God formed man from the dust of the ground and breathed into his nostrils the breath or spirit of life, and man became a living being.

Even though God spoke to them in Genesis 1:28-29, He did not create their bodies until Genesis 2:7. This proves that we are spiritual as well as physical beings. If we live our lives focused only upon the human part of us, we will miss all that God has for us. Read Genesis 2:7 again and notice that God breathes the "spirit of life" into man—putting into a human body the same spirit He is addressing in Genesis 1:28-29.

In fact, the Bible is full of scriptures that prove we are body, soul, and spirit. Here are just a few:

And may the God of peace Himself sanctify you through and through [*separate you from profane things, make you pure and wholly consecrated to God*]; and may your spirit and soul and body be preserved sound and complete [*and found*] blameless at the coming of our Lord Jesus Christ (the Messiah).

I Thess. 5:23 (**The Amplified Bible**)

For the Word that God speaks is alive and full of power [*making it active, operative, energizing, and effective*]; it is sharper than any two-edged sword, penetrating to the dividing line of the breath of life (soul) and [*the immortal*] spirit, and of joints and marrow [*of the deepest parts of our nature*], exposing and sifting and analyzing and judging the very thoughts and purposes of the heart.

Heb. 4:12 (**The Amplified Bible**)

Therefore we do not become discouraged (utterly spiritless, exhausted, and wearied out through fear). Though our outer man is [*progressively*] decaying and wasting away, yet our inner self is being [*progressively*] renewed day after day.

II Co. 4:16 (**The Amplified Bible**)

Let's look at the three parts of man so you can better understand how this concept works.

BODY

The body is the part of us that everyone is familiar with. God created our bodies so we could function here on earth. Each of us is unique; no two people on the face of the earth are alike. We all have our own DNA, fingerprint, and heartbeat.

It is this body that uses the five senses: touch, taste, smell, sight, and hearing. God gave us these senses to help us function in this world. Our physical body will not leave this world; it was created to function only here. Think of it as your "Earth suit," much like the space suit that astronauts must wear when they go to the moon.

In order to understand spiritual things, however, you must move beyond the concerns of your physical body. Let's look at what Paul tells the Corinthian church about having a carnal mind:

> **However, brethren, I could not talk to you as to spiritual [*men*], but as to nonspiritual [*men of the flesh, in whom the carnal nature predominates*], as to mere infants [*in the new life*] in Christ [*unable to talk yet!*] I fed you with milk, not solid food, for you were not yet strong enough [*to be ready for it*]; but even yet you are not strong enough [*to be ready for it*], for you are still [*unspiritual, having the nature*] of the flesh [*under the control of ordinary impulses*]. For as long as [*there are*] envying and jealousy and wrangling and factions among you, are you not unspiritual and of the flesh, behaving yourselves after a human standard and like mere (unchanged) men?**
>
> I Co. 3:1-3 (**The Amplified Bible**)

Paul is asking the Corinthians to get beyond the human part of them and to move toward things of God, which are spiritual. As long as you focus only on your human needs, you will never understand the spiritual.

SOUL

The soul is the inner life of a person, the seat of our emotions and the center of our personality. Without the soul, the body would be only as valuable as the dirt from which it was created. Like the body, the soul also has five senses: imagination, conscience, memory, reason, and affection. Remember that in Genesis 2:7, God breathes the spirit of life into man to create a living soul. Therefore, the soul can also be considered the natural part of man. Let's read what Paul tells the Corinthian church about the "natural man":

> **But the natural, nonspiritual man does not accept or welcome or admit into his heart the gifts and teachings and revelations of the Spirit of God, for they are folly (meaningless nonsense) to him; and he is incapable of knowing them [*of progressively recognizing, understanding, and becoming better acquainted with them*] because they are spiritually discerned and estimated and appreciated.**

> **I Co. 2:14 (The Amplified Bible)**

Paul is telling the Corinthians that the natural man—the human soul—does not accept or welcome spiritual understanding. Why? Because of Adam's sin in the Garden of Eden. I will explain this in more detail later in this chapter.

SPIRIT

The spirit is the immaterial, invisible part of man. The spirit is like the wind: we can't see it, but we know it's real. The spirit also has five senses: faith, hope, reverence, prayer, and worship.

The spirit is the part of us that God deals with; it is our spirit that He seeks. He wants to have a real relationship with the part of us that is eternal, like Him, and He wants to put our spirit to His purpose. Paul tells the Corinthians that God has revealed His plans for us by His spirit in I Corinthians 2:9-12

> **But, on the contrary, as the Scripture says, What eye has not seen and ear has not heard and has not entered into the heart of man, [*all that*] God has prepared (made and keeps ready) for those who love Him [*who hold Him in affectionate reverence, promptly obeying Him and gratefully recognizing the benefits He has bestowed*]. Yet to us God has unveiled and revealed them by and through His Spirit, for the [*Holy*] Spirit searches diligently, exploring and examining everything, even sounding the profound and bottomless things of God [*the divine counsels and things hidden and beyond man's scrutiny*]. For what person perceives (knows and understands) what passes through a man's thoughts except the man's own spirit within him? Just so no one discerns (comes to know and comprehend) the thoughts of God except the Spirit of God. Now we have not received the spirit [*that belongs to*] the world, but the [*Holy*] Spirit Who is from God, [*given to us*] that we might realize and comprehend and appreciate the gifts [*of divine favor and blessing so freely and lavishly*] bestowed on us by God.**

Again, Paul is telling the Corinthians that they can know God's purpose for their lives if they receive His spirit in their spirit.

God wants you to become spiritually pregnant with His plans for your life.

Genesis 1:26-28 describes God's perfect union with man. In the Garden, He came down from heaven every day and communed with Adam and Eve. He gave them clear instructions for how to live, but they didn't listen, and man fell. In his unfallen state, the spirit of man was illuminated from heaven. But when the human race fell in the person of Adam, sin closed the window of the spirit. Man's heart remained unregenerate until Jesus Christ came and gave His life.

We see now why the natural man cannot understand spiritual things: he cannot understand them until his spiritual nature has been renewed.

RECEIVING JESUS AS LORD AND SAVIOR

Remember, if a woman is going to become pregnant, there must be a union of sperm and egg. The same is true in the spiritual sense. If we are going to become pregnant in spirit, there must be a union between us and God, a union accomplished by accepting Jesus as our Lord and savior. Let's look at Romans 8:8-10 to see how this happens:

So then those who are living the life of the flesh [*catering to the appetites and impulses of their carnal nature*] cannot please or satisfy God, or be acceptable to Him. But you are not living the life of the flesh, you are living the life of the Spirit, if the [*Holy*] Spirit of God [*really*] dwells within you [*directs and controls you*]. But if anyone does not possess the [*Holy*] Spirit of Christ, he is none of His [*he does not belong to Christ, is not truly a child of God*]. But if Christ lives in you, [*then although*] your

11

[*natural*] **body is dead by reason of sin and guilt, the spirit is alive because of [*the*] righteousness [*that He imputes to you*].**

Paul is explaining here how to receive salvation. He is letting us know that all we need to do is confess Jesus as our Lord and savior—to believe in our heart—and we are saved. I must tell you that you will never become pregnant with God's purpose until you marry Him, because God doesn't fool around. He doesn't want a part-time lover, and he doesn't want to be your sugar daddy. It's all or nothing.

Once you receive Jesus as your savior, you are married into the body of Christ. You are now in position for the next step.

Remember that in order for pregnancy to occur, there must be an egg and sperm. Well, you have the egg, and God has the sperm. In order for Him to get the sperm to you, one more thing must take place: you have to receive the gift of the Holy Spirit. It is this Spirit that God uses to get you pregnant. Let's look at the scriptures to see how this works:

But while he thought on these things, behold, the angel of the Lord appeared unto him in a dream, saying, Joseph, thou son of David, fear not to take unto thee Mary thou wife: for that which is conceived in her is of the Holy Ghost. And she shall bring forth a son, and thou shalt call his name Jesus: for he shall save his people from their sins.

Matt. 1:20-21 (King James Bible)

In this passage, the angel is talking to Joseph because he thought that Mary had been unfaithful to him by getting pregnant before they married, which was a crime punishable by death. The angel is explaining that the baby Mary is carrying is of the Holy Ghost. Now, I know that Jesus was a real baby, but God used the Spirit to impregnate Mary.

Let's look at this story in a broader sense. Whenever God impregnates you with His purpose, it is the Spirit that performs the task. Just like Mary, we are living in the time of the Holy Spirit. Consider how Mary conceived the baby: the Spirit overtook her. You need the same thing to happen in your life if God is going to use you; the Spirit must overtake you. Before He trusted her with such an awesome responsibility, Mary was in good fellowship with God. Because of that, she was able to conceive.

Next we'll see what the Bible says about receiving the Holy Spirit.

RECEIVING THE HOLY SPIRIT

And it came to pass, that, while Apollos was at Corinth, Paul having passed through the upper coast came to Ephesus, and finding certain disciples, He said unto them, have ye received the Holy Ghost since ye believe? And they said unto him, we have not so much as heard whether there be any Holy Ghost. And he said unto them, unto what then were ye baptized? And they said, unto John's baptism. Then said Paul, John verily baptized with the baptism of repentance, saying unto the people, that

they should believe in him which should come after him, that is, in Christ Jesus.

When they heard this, they were baptized in the name of the Lord Jesus. And when Paul had laid his hand upon them, the Holy Ghost came on them; and they spake with tongues, and prophesied.

Acts 19:1-6 (King James Bible)

Paul explains here that after the apostles received Jesus as their savior, they needed to take the next step and receive the gift of the Holy Spirit. After hearing about the Spirit, they gladly received Him and began to speak in tongues. If you are going to conceive God's plan for your life, you must have the Holy Spirit, who will impregnate you with purpose.

Consider what Jesus told Nicodemus about the "born again" experience:

There was a man of the Pharisees, named Nicodemus, a ruler of the Jews: The same came to Jesus by night, and said unto him, Rabbi, we know that thou are a teacher come from God: for no man can do these miracles that thou doest, except God be with him. Jesus answered and said unto him, verily, verily, I say unto thee, except a man be born again, he cannot see the kingdom of God. Nicodemus said unto him, how can a man be born again when he is old? Can he enter a second time into his mother's womb, and be born? Jesus answered, verily, verily, I say unto thee, except a man be born of water and of the Spirit, he cannot

enter into the kingdom of God. That which is born of the flesh is flesh; and that which is born of the Spirit is Spirit. Marvel not that I said unto thee, ye must be born again.

John 3:1-7 (King James Bible)

In this text, Jesus is telling Nicodemus that there is no way he can enter into God's way of doing things unless he is born again. Notice the first thing Jesus says: only someone who is born again can see God's kingdom. If you are going to see the kingdom—God's way of doing things—you must marry Him. By doing this, your eyes will be opened to His ways. Next Jesus says that someone can't enter the kingdom unless he is born again. In other words, not only won't you see God's ways, but you also won't walk in His ways. In order to walk you must see where you're going, and you can only do this by receiving Jesus as your Lord and Savior. This will open your heart, making it ready for God's seed.

Nicodemus thought that his education and position in society made him a prime candidate for the Lord's blessing. He was one of the leaders of his day; surely this made him ready and worthy to carry God's baby. However, it is not education or status that readies you for spiritual conception, but your relationship with God. This world is full of people who don't understand this, who don't have a clue what they are supposed to be doing.

CONSUMMATION

After you have received Jesus as your savior and received the gift of the Holy Spirit, you must make your union with God complete by consummating the marriage. You do this by having a prayer life. The more time you spend with the Lord, the closer you will get to Him, and the only way you can get to know your mate is to spend time with Him. It is during these times of prayer that God will tell you what He likes and you can tell Him what you like. The coming together in prayer will make the two become one, setting the stage for conception.

These are some beautiful times. In Jewish custom, a newly married couple would take one whole year off from work to spend with one another. In the same way, you should spend some time with Jesus so He can love on you as only He can. He longs to love you and spend quality time telling you how crazy He is about you. He wants to whisper in your ear and tell you that you're all His and that He will never leave you. He wants to surprise you with gifts He picked out just for you.

Take a minute right now to love on Jesus. Tell Him how much you love Him and how much He means to you. Can't you feel his presence coming into the room? Take some time now and let Him have His way—you won't regret it.

You can now see that a few things must take place before you can conceive God's plans for your life:

1. You must receive Jesus as your Lord and Savior.
2. You must receive the gift of the Holy Spirit.

3. You must consummate the relationship.

Finally, always remember the night you got married to Jesus—the wedding was beautiful. You had accepted the marriage proposal from Jesus, and the wedding was on. Jesus was the groom, you were the bride, the Spirit gave you away, and God performed the wedding. It was a magical night, just you and Jesus all alone. He told you how much He loved you, and you reciprocated. Then you got together, and when He came into you, He deposited the gift of the Holy Spirit, and you conceived.

Chapter Two

PREGNANCY TEST

One of the first signs of pregnancy is when a woman misses her menstrual period. Others symptoms include breast tenderness and swelling, fatigue, nausea, sensitivity to smell, increased frequency of urination, mood swings, and the most obvious symptom, weight gain. Some women even experience unusual cravings. When these signs appear, it is a good idea for the woman to have a test done to find out if she is carrying a baby.

There are many ways to take a pregnancy test, but in general, you can either go to your physician or take an over-the-counter test. If you go to the doctor, he will test your blood; if you take the home test, you will test your urine. This is how to determine if the physical body is pregnant. Detecting a spiritual pregnancy, however, is quite different; it is not the body but the life that goes through telltale changes. To see if you are pregnant in the spirit, you can go to your doctor, Jesus, or take a home test. I'll warn you that the home test is rarely reliable—but Jesus is 100 percent accurate.

HOME TEST

The home test for spiritual pregnancy involves asking other people about your future and hoping that they can give you good advice. There are some problems with this test: all people tend to see life from their own limited perspective, most people don't want to see you get too far ahead of them, and some people will simply give you the wrong advice.

The best way to find out if you are pregnant is to go to Dr. Jesus; He can tell you the purpose for which you were created. After all, according to Genesis 1:26-27, God created man in His image. And the best way to find out something's purpose is to talk to its creator.

Here's what the Bible says:

Trust in the Lord with all thine heart; and lean not unto thine own understanding, in all thy ways acknowledge Him, and He shall direct thy path

Prov. 3:5-6 (King James Bible)

It is God's desire to lead you in the way that He would have you go, but you must put your trust in Him. He is the one who made you, and He can lead you down the right path.

SIGNS OF SPIRITUAL PREGNANCY

One of the first signs of physical pregnancy is a missed menstrual period—the monthly bleeding stops. Have your periods of bleeding stopped? Have you stopped the known sins in your life? When a woman is pregnant, her body stops the cycle because there is a change taking place within her, and even the body knows that in order to bring in the new, you have to change the normal way of doing things. This is also true in the spiritual sense. When you are pregnant spiritually, things must change.

In Genesis 32:24-31, Jacob wrestles with an angel all night until the angel blesses him. In this story we see God changing the normal cycle of Jacob's life because Jacob is pregnant with purpose. We see this pattern repeated throughout the Bible as God breaks the cycles in the lives of people like Abraham, Sarah, Peter, and Saul (Paul).

A second sign of physical pregnancy is that a woman's breasts swell and become tender, as the parts of her that will eventually feed the baby get ready to carry the milk they will need to do so. Spiritually, our ears serve that purpose, desiring the word of God and swelling with the knowledge of it. But James 2:22-26 says to be doers of the Word, and not just hearers:

> You see that [*his*] faith was cooperating with his works, and [*his*] faith was completed and reached its supreme expression [*when he implemented it*] by [*good*] works. And [*so*] the Scripture was fulfilled that says, Abraham believed in (adhered to, trusted in, and relied on) God, and this was accounted to him as righteousness (as conformity to God's will in thought and deed), and he was called God's friend. You see that a man is justified (pronounced righteous before God) through what he does and not alone through faith [*through works of obedience as well as by what he believes*]. So also with Rahab the harlot—was she not shown to be justified (pronounced righteous before God) by [*good*] deeds when she took in the scouts (spies) and sent them away by a different route? [*Josh. 2:1-21.*] For as the human body apart from the spirit is lifeless, so faith apart from [*its*] works of obedience is also dead.

You need to study God's word so that when the time comes, you can be ready to feed your purpose with scripture.

The more of the Word you know, the more able you will be to do the Lord's will. Put your ears to God's mouth and let them swell with His word. By doing this, you will have more than enough nourishment to feed your baby, called Purpose.

The next sign of physical pregnancy is frequent urination. Just as a pregnant woman must keep going to the restroom to release the built-up water, you should always be releasing the extra stuff in your life. There should be times when you let go of some friends, lovers, jobs, and family members—anything or anyone that threatens to drown your purpose.

The next thing that a pregnant woman can experience is mood swings. Because of the changes to her body, she might feel happy one minute and sad the next. And that's normal—it's the baby inside her body that's causing her change of moods. If you have mood swings that you can't explain, you could be spiritually pregnant. Whenever God's mood changes, His "move" changes. That's why you are going through all the mood swings, so He can move you to the place where He wants you to be.

The most obvious sign of physical pregnancy is weight gain, as the woman begins to "eat for two"—and the more food she eats, the more weight she gains. It's the law of deposit: whenever you make a deposit into something, it will grow or enlarge. Similarly, if you are spiritually pregnant, you should be gaining weight. The difference is that the weight you gain will be in your head, not your body. You must become a spiritual heavyweight, and the only way to do this is to study God's word until you expand in the spirit. That is why you need to attend church and Bible class regularly.

The last symptom a pregnant woman can experience is cravings. She can desire all types of food at all times of day, and she won't be satisfied until her cravings are met. Maybe you find yourself not getting enough of the word of God—you desire it day and night, and it can't come fast enough. Your craving of the Word is being enhanced by your faith, and you are experiencing all sorts of unusual feelings. This is a good indication that something inside you needs more nourishment than you normally feed it. Could you be spiritually pregnant?

The Bible tells us of many people who went through some of the spiritual symptoms I just mentioned. As you read some of their stories, below, see if you can tell how their pregnancy tests came out.

NOW [*in Haran*] the Lord said to Abram, Go for yourself [*for your own advantage*] away from your country, from your relatives and your father's house, to the land that I will show you. And I will make of you a great nation, and I will bless you [*with abundant increase of favors*] and make your name famous and distinguished, and you will be a blessing [*dispensing good to others*]. And I will bless those who bless you [*who confer prosperity or happiness upon you*] and curse him who curses or uses insolent language toward you; in you will all the families and kindred of the earth be blessed [*and by you they will bless themselves*].

Gen. 12:1-3 (The Amplified Bible)

Here you see God giving Abram his life purpose, instructing him to move away from everything he knows to a new place that God will show him. Abram grew up in a city called Ur, where the people did not worship the Lord, so God is separating Abram from people who will hinder His plans for Abram. Then the Lord promises Abram a great future and tells him that he will receive supernatural protection. God is promising all this to see if Abram will trust Him and move out on faith. Sometimes the Lord will do the same thing in your life, to see if you have the faith you say you do. To see where your heart is, He will ask you to leave things behind. How many times have you had to let go of some things that you knew were just dragging you down? Lot, one of the only family members who went with Abram, eventually had to leave him.

In Genesis 17:4-5, God confirms his promise to Abram:

As for me, behold, my covenant is with thee, and thou shalt be a father of many nations. Neither shall thou name anymore be called Abram, but thou name shall be called Abraham; for a father of many nations have I made thee.

Here God is letting Abram know that He is a God of His word—when God tells you something, you can take it to the bank. And notice that God has just changed Abram's name to Abraham, meaning "father of many nations."

In order to get God's blessing in your life, you must make some changes. By asking Abram to move away and change his name, God is preparing him for the future.

If you continue to read the story of Abraham, you will see all kinds of changes take place in his life. One of the biggest tests Abraham has to face is when he is asked to do something that will forever set his destiny. Let's look at the story in Genesis 22 to see the test Abraham is given:

And it came to pass after these things, that God did tempt Abraham, and said unto him, Abraham: and he said, behold, here I am. And he said, take now thy son, thine only son Isaac, whom thou lovest, and get thee into the land of moriah; and offer him there for a burnt offering upon one of the mountains which I will tell thee of. And Abraham rose up early in the morning, and saddled his ass, and took two of his young men with him, and Isaac his son, and clave the wood for the burnt-offering, and rose up, and went unto the place of which God had told him. Then on the third day Abraham lifted up his eyes, and saw the place afar off. And Abraham said unto his young men, abide ye here with the ass, and I and the lad will go yonder and worship, and come again to you. And Abraham took the wood of the burnt—offering, and laid it upon Isaac his son, and he took the fire in his hand, and a knife; and they went both of them together. And Isaac spake unto Abraham his father, and said, my father: and he said, here am I, my son. And he said behold the fire and the wood: but where is the lamb for the burnt-offering? And Abraham said, my son, God will provide himself a lamb for the burnt-offering: so they went both of them together. And they came to the place which God had told him of; and Abraham built an altar there, and laid the wood in order, and bound Isaac his son, and laid him on the altar upon the wood. And Abraham stretched forth his hand, and took the knife to slay his son. And the angel of the Lord called unto him out of the heaven, and said, Abraham, Abraham: and he said, here am I. And he said, lay not thy hand upon the lad, neither do thy anything unto him: for now I know that thou fearest God, seeing that thou has not withheld thy son, thine only son from me.

Gen. 22:1-12 (King James Bible)

In this story, you see God asking Abraham to give up—to kill—the one thing that he had waited for all his life: his son, Isaac. God is testing Abraham to see if he will be faithful to Him with all that he has. Let's be honest for a moment here—how many of us would willingly give up our only son or the one thing that we love more than anything else? There will be times when God will test your faith in Him, as he did Abraham's; I believe that God wanted to know if Isaac meant more to Abraham than He did. Remember that whatever is closer to you than God is also closer to God than you are. There must never be anything in your life that you aren't willing to give to God. He must always come first, before anyone else. Abraham passed his test with flying colors; he was now ready to leap right into his future.

Now let's see if you can recognize some of the symptoms of pregnancy in Abraham's life. Remember the signs—a missed menstrual period, breast tenderness and swelling, fatigue, nausea, frequent urination, mood swings, and weight gain. If you read Abraham's story, I believe you'll see that all those symptoms are present. God breaks the cycle of sin in his life by moving him away from his family, friends, and loved ones, and so his bleeding stops. God prepares Abraham for his life purpose by revealing Himself to him; this knowledge of God causes a swelling to take place in Abraham's life. The more Abraham knows about God, the more tender his life becomes and the readier he is to feed his future. Abraham also begins to experience fatigue with his situation; sometimes he is weighed down by the burden of God's promise, his future as the father of many nations. He feels so weighed down, in fact, that he and his wife get together and come up with a plan to help God out. Let's look at Genesis to see what they do:

> Now Sarai, Abram's wife, had borne him no children. She had an Egyptian maid whose name was Hagar. And Sarai said to Abram, See here, the Lord has restrained me from bearing [*children*]. I am asking you to have intercourse with my maid; it may be that I can obtain children by her. And Abram listened to and heeded what Sarai said. So Sarai, Abram's wife, took Hagar her Egyptian maid, after Abram had dwelt ten years in the land of Canaan, and gave her to her husband Abram to be his [*secondary*] wife. And he had intercourse with Hagar, and she became pregnant; and when she saw that she was with child, she looked with contempt upon her mistress and despised her.

Gen. 16:1-4 (The Amplified Bible)

In this passage, we see Abraham and Sarai deciding that God is taking too long to fulfill His promise, so Abraham lies with Hager, Sarai's servant, who gives birth to Ishmael.

I have to pause here and say that God will never bless your mess—He will only bless your obedience.

Abraham also begins to feel nauseated at times, when the things going on around him make him want to throw up. Could this have been spiritual morning sickness? This is how you should feel if you are pregnant—there should be things that you used to do that you just can't do anymore, and when you're around them, you feel sick. And then the Bible tells us of times when Abraham feels the need to let some things go. This is spiritual equivalent of frequent urination, such as when Abraham must separate himself from Lot.

Let's look at the story in Genesis:

> **But Lot, who went with Abram, also had flocks and herds and tents.**
>
> **Now the land was not able to nourish and support them so they could dwell together, for their possessions were too great for them to live together. And there was strife between the herdsmen of Abram's cattle and the herdsmen of Lot's cattle. And the Canaanite and the Perizzite were dwelling then in the land [*making fodder more difficult to obtain*].**
>
> **So Abram said to Lot, Let there be no strife, I beg of you, between you and me, or between your herdsmen and my herdsmen, for we are relatives. Is not the whole land before you? Separate yourself, I beg of you, from me. If you take the left hand, then I will go to the right; or if you choose the right hand, then I will go to the left.**
>
> **Gen. 13:5-9 (The Amplified Bible)**

At this point Abraham (Abram) and Lot are so blessed that the land is not able to bear them, so they have to separate. When God blesses you there will not be room enough to bear all those blessings. There was an abundance of blessing going on in Abraham's life, so he had to release the overflow. God wants to bless you to the point where you'll have to give something away.

I know that there are all kinds of things going on in your life right now, and you feel like you don't know what to do and no one understands, but this is the time to release some things, to let them go. There is a purpose in you that can't share the space, so you will have to make a choice. God and the devil can never be roommates.

Abraham also experienced mood swings—the emotional roller coaster ride that goes along with great change. One moment he had all the faith in the world, and the next he wasn't sure what was going on. When you read Abraham's story, you can see that he is far more stable at some times than at others.

Have you ever felt like Dr. Jekyll and Mr. Hyde—one moment you know exactly who you are, and the next, you don't? Sometimes you experience so many life changes that you don't even act the same anymore. Be honest with yourself for a moment: you don't like every change that the Lord makes in your life, do you? I know people who walk around, especially in church, acting like they have it all under control, when the truth is they're not in control—God is, and His will sometime causes emotional ups and downs. Can you imagine the mood swings Abraham went through when God finally gave him a son, just to turn around and ask Abraham to kill him?

What life changes are you going through? What are you being asked to give up? How are you expected to act, and where are you expected to be? There are a million questions going through your mind right now, and you don't know how to answer them. No wonder your moods keep changing! Put your trust in God, the Bible says, and He will lead you down the right path.

Trust in the Lord with all thine heart; and lean not unto thy own understanding. In all thy ways acknowledge him, and he shall direct thy paths.

Prov. 3:5-6 (King James Bible)

Over the course of Abraham's story, you can see him begin to gain some spiritual weight. With every trial he faces, he goes up another level in his relationship with the Lord. By the end of his life, Abraham has become one of the biblical figures known for their awesome faith. It was by this faith that he grew bigger and bigger in the Lord until he had gained enough weight to feed a nation.

These are times when you might feel overwhelmed by change on multiple levels. Your life is changing, your feelings are changing, your surroundings are changing, your mind is changing, and you feel weighed down by all of the changes. Just remember one thing: before having a baby, you have to gain the right amount of weight. In the same way, before you can work for the Lord, He needs you to gain some spiritual weight. Just think what would happen if a lightweight were to get into the ring with Mike

Tyson—Tyson would kill the guy. The same thing is true with spiritual battles; the devil will kill every lightweight who gets into the ring with him.

Cravings are the surest sign that something profound is happening inside you. You begin to experience a deep desire for holy things. The older Abraham got, the more he desired the will of the Lord. Do you find yourself wanting more and more of the word of God, to the point that it can't come fast enough? This is a sign that there is something in you longing for satisfaction. It's a craving that can be satisfied only by the one who put it there, God.

I believe you can tell by the events of Abraham's life that he was indeed spiritually pregnant. Let's look for similar symptoms in the life of another of God's servants, Saul, to see if he passed the pregnancy test:

And Saul, yet breathing out threatening and slaughter against the disciples of the Lord, went unto the high priest, and desired of him letters to Damascus to the synagogues, that if he found any of this way, whether they were men or women, he might bring them bound unto Jerusalem. And as he journeyed, he came near Damascus: and suddenly there shined round about him a light from heaven: And he fell to the earth, and heard a voice saying unto him, Saul, Saul, why persecuted thou me? And he said, who art thou, Lord? And the Lord said, I am Jesus whom thy persecutest: it is hard for thee to kick against the pricks. And he trembling and astonished said, Lord, what will thou have me to do? And the Lord said unto him,

arise, and go into the city, and it shall be told thee what thou must do.

Acts 9:1-6 (King James Bible)

Here you see Saul doing everything in his power to kill anyone who accepted Jesus as his savior. And he truly believed that he was doing the right thing by killing Christians; he had gotten his orders, and off he went, killing any Christian in his path. Saul had grown up a religious man and was trained by the best. No one could tell him that he wasn't doing the world a favor by ridding it of all of the believers.

At one point, Saul witnesses the killing of Stephen:

Now upon hearing these things, they [*the Jews*] were cut to the heart and infuriated, and they ground their teeth against [*Stephen*]. But he, full of the Holy Spirit and controlled by Him, gazed into heaven and saw the glory (the splendor and majesty) of God, and Jesus standing at God's right hand; and he said, Look! I see the heavens opened, and the Son of man standing at God's right hand! But they raised a great shout and put their hands over their ears and rushed together upon him. Then they dragged him out of the city and began to stone him, and the witnesses placed their garments at the feet of a young man named Saul. And while they were stoning Stephen, he prayed, Lord Jesus, receive and accept and welcome my spirit!

Acts 7:54-59 (The Amplified Bible)

As other men stoned Stephen, Saul stood there, holding their coats. Everything in Saul's life, from his early childhood up to this point, only served to strengthen his belief in tradition.

I would say that Saul took a home pregnancy test—that is, everything he did was validated by man, not God. You need to remember that *tradition is the enemy of revelation.* The more you do to please man, the more you will displease God. A home pregnancy test will have you asking friends, family, and loved ones—everyone but God—about your future. At this point in his life, Saul was pleasing everyone but the Lord. I'm sure he had his whole life mapped out: where he would go to school, where he would live, what kind of woman he would marry, the kind of house he would buy, how many kids he would have, the type of job he would have, the clubs he would belong to, how many promotions he would get . . . he probably even tried to plan how long he would live. It's easy to see how a home pregnancy test can mislead you; you run around, telling everyone things that aren't true, because you got too excited check with the doctor first.

Fortunately, since Saul didn't check with the doctor first, the doctor made a house call. Jesus stopped Saul right in his tracks and questioned him about the things he was doing. Jesus told Saul that it would be hard for him to stop the momentum of the church, and then He began to let Saul know the real purpose of his life.

Let's look more closely at Saul's story to see how his pregnancy test turned out. In the text below, you'll see that God stops the regular cycle of Saul's life on the road to Damascus. Saul had a history of killing Christians, and if the Lord was going to use him, He had to break that cycle. Remember that a missed menstrual cycle is one of the first signs of pregnancy; it's an interruption in the regular course of things. And then there is another significant symptom, breast tenderness and swelling. It was time for Saul to become sensitive to the word of God, to swell with the Holy Ghost. Read Acts 9:7-17 to see how this happened:

> **And the men which journeyed with him stood speechless, hearing a voice, but seeing no man. And Saul arose from the earth; and when his eyes were opened, he saw no man: but they led him by the hand, and brought him into Damascus. And he was three days without sight, and neither did he eat or drink. And there was a certain disciple at Damascus, named Ananias; and to him said the Lord in a vision, Ananias, and he said, behold, I am here, Lord. And the Lord said unto him, arise, and go into the street which is called straight, and enquire in the house of Judas for one called Saul, of Tarsus: for, behold, he prayeth. And has seen in a vision a man named Ananias. Coming in, and putting his hand on him, that he might receive his sight. Then Ananias answered, Lord, I have heard by many of this man, how much evil he has done to thy saints at Jerusalem: And here he has authority from the chief priest to bind all that call on thy name. But the Lord said unto him, go thou way: for he is a chosen vessel unto me, to bear my name before the Gentiles, and kings, and the children of Israel: For I will show him how great things he must suffer for my name's sake. And Ananias went**

his way, and entered into the house; and putting his hands on him said, brother Saul, the Lord, even Jesus, that appeared unto thee in the way as thy camest, hath sent me, that thou mightest receive thou sight, and be filled with the Holy Ghost.

Jesus brought Saul through all those tender moments to fill him with the spirit so that Saul would trust Him as Lord and savior. With all the changes taking place, you can imagine the fatigue that Saul felt; the Bible indicates as much in Acts 19, when Saul receives meat and is strengthened. No doubt he felt spiritual as well as physical fatigue.

After the changes in Saul's life, including his name change to Paul, he became more sensitive to the movement of the spirit, and that made it hard for him to keep doing the things he was used to doing. Paul was so committed to the cause of Christ that whenever he was around sin, it bothered him; you might say it made him nauseated. That's what sin should do in your life: when you're around it, you should feel sick. This happens because you are a new creature, as the Bible explains in 2 Corinthians 5:17:

Therefore if any man be in Christ, he is a new creature: old things are passed away; behold, all things are become new.

As a Christian, Paul continually made changes in his life, always eliminating things that were not in keeping with the life of Christ, just as a pregnant woman frequently relieves herself of extra fluid. This is the same thing you must do in your life. If you are truly spiritually pregnant, there should be a release of sin from your life.

With the exception of Jesus, God worked more through Paul than through anyone else in the New Testament. Paul's life was filled with ups and downs, but by the end of his life, you can see that God used him mightily. It's safe to say that Paul was truly pregnant for the Lord.

We've looked at just two biblical examples of men who were truly pregnant for the Lord. You saw all the changes that were made in their lives and how the Lord used them mightily. If you want God to use you mightily, make sure that you go to the real doctor for your pregnancy test. God is the only one who can reveal to you the real purpose for your life, because He is your creator and ruler. If you are experiencing missed cycles, breast tenderness, swelling, fatigue, nausea, frequent urination, mood swings, weight gain, and cravings—get excited! God is preparing you for your true life purpose.

CHAPTER THREE
DIET

Congratulations! I trust that you are moving on to this chapter because you have confirmed that you are pregnant. Isn't it exciting! Just think—God trusts you with His baby, named Purpose. This is an awesome responsibility; He could have picked anyone to do what He trusts you to do. Don't take it lightly. There is something inside you, a special purpose that only you can do. This is the reason you were born.

That's what makes this chapter extremely important. Whenever a woman finds out that she is pregnant, her doctor monitors her diet. What she eats is extremely important to the health of her baby. Everything that goes in her mouth will affect not just her health, but also the health of her child. It is important, therefore, that she gets all the necessary vitamins and other nourishment. The same thing is true when you are spiritually pregnant: the health of your baby depends on what you eat. *What a woman eats physically affects her baby, but what she eats spiritually affects her future.*

UMBILICAL CORD

A pregnant woman feeds her baby through an umbilical cord, a long, flexible cord which provides the fetus nourishment as it grows and develops within the uterus. One end of the cord attaches to the baby's abdominal area; the other end attaches to the placenta, where the blood vessels of the mother and baby exchange the contents of their circulatory systems. Two large arteries in the umbilical cord deliver oxygen and nutrients from the placenta to the fetus, while a large vein carries carbon dioxide and other wastes from the fetus to the placenta. Most of these wastes are transferred to the mother's bloodstream and eliminated through her excretory system.

The mother and her child are intricately interconnected. This is why her diet is so important; everything she eats will be passed along to the baby. At the same time, an emotional bond is forming between them because of the dependence of the child upon the mother.

The same dynamic occurs with a spiritual pregnancy. You should be connected to the Lord for your nourishment. That's why it is now important that you know the word of the Lord and feed on it daily.

In Proverbs 3:1-8, we are instructed to take God's word seriously:

> **My son, forget not my law; but let thy heart keep my commandments: For length of days, and long life, and peace, shall they add to thee. Let not mercy and truth forsake thee: bind them about thy neck; write them upon the tables of thine heart: So shalt thou find favor and good understanding in the sight of God and men. Trust in the Lord with all thine heart; and lean not unto thy own understanding. In all of thy ways acknowledge him, and he shall direct thy paths. Be not wise in thy own eyes: fear the Lord, and depart from evil. It shall be health to thy navel, and marrow to thy bones.**

Solomon is instructing you here never to forget the Word, because it will feed your destiny. If you follow the word of the Lord, He promises to bless you. And notice Solomon's use of language in this passage; he says that God's word, if followed, will be health to your navel and marrow to your bones. Just as physical nourishment travels through the umbilical cord from mother to child, spiritual nourishment travels through the Word from God's mouth to your ears. You will get all the nourishment you need from the Word, so monitor your diet and make sure you're getting a healthy portion of it. The more Word you know, the healthier your future will be.

We are encouraged to study in 2 Timothy 2:15:

Study to show thyself approved unto God, a workman that needeth not to be ashamed, rightly dividing the word of truth.

At times you will want to eat junk food, but remember: the more junk you eat, the more junk your baby eats, too. The spiritual equivalent of junk food is a misinterpretation of the Word or a watered-down sermon. That's why it's important that you study for yourself, to make sure that you're receiving God's word and no one else's. The health of your baby is so important—before you eat anything, check the label first!

Your diet is critical now. You have someone else to think about, so you can't just eat whatever you want. Everything you do now is important and will shape the new life inside you; everything you watch on television and listen to on the radio will affect your future. *Your destiny will be only as strong as what you feed it.*

The devil will now begin to tempt you with drugs and alcohol, because he wants you to have a crack baby. He knows that if he can get you hooked on something, your baby will be hooked, too. Whatever purpose God has for you doesn't just affect you; it affects everyone else. And whatever you get hooked on won't just affect you; it will also affect the baby you're carrying.

I'm talking about sin. It will cause you to lose your baby.

To see what God says about this, let's look at the story of Israel in Ezekiel 16:1-4:

Again the word of the Lord came unto me, saying, Son of man, cause Jerusalem to know her abominations, And say, thus saith the Lord God unto Jerusalem; thy birth and thy nativity is of the land of Canaan; thy father was an Amorite, and thy mother a Hittite. And as for thy nativity, in the day thou were born thy navel was not cut, neither were thou washed in water to supply thee; thou was not salted at all, nor swaddled at all.

The Lord is telling Ezekiel that the children of Israel did not listen to His commandments, and by doing this they were like malnourished babies. God did not want the Israelites to marry people from other traditions; He wanted their customs to stay pure. I know that this seems trivial, but think about it for a minute—when you marry someone from another tradition, one of two things will happen: you will change him, or he will change you. The Lord knew that the latter would happen—and that's true in the spiritual sense, too. God does not want you playing around with the devil and his devices.

Once a child is born, the umbilical cord must be cut—the child can't go through life attached to his mother.

Shortly after delivery, the cord is clamped in two places and severed between the clamps. The infant is thereby separated from the placenta and from that point on is not fed that way again. In the same way, the Lord tells Jerusalem that it's time to cut the umbilical cord. I've spent all this time nourishing you, He says, and you should now be ready to eat. Instead, you're still acting like unborn babies.

That's why it is extremely important that you learn the word of the Lord. As long as you stay hooked up to God, you will get all the nourishment you need to have a healthy baby. The Word will facilitate your growth process. Here's what Paul says about growing up in the Lord:

When I was a child, I spake as a child, I understood as a child, I thought as a child: but when I became a man, I put away childish things.

1Cor. 13:11 (King James Bible)

If you're pregnant and your diet is right, your baby will develop at a normal rate, but if your diet is not right, your baby will be malnourished, and babies born malnourished must be put on life support. At every stage of pregnancy, the diet should meet the needs of the child.

That's what Paul says in Hebrews 5:11-14—that in order to grow up in the Lord, you must eat a healthy portion of God's word daily:

Of whom we have many things to say, and hard to be uttered, seeing ye are hard of hearing. For

when for the times ye ought to be teachers, ye have need that one teach you again which be the first principles of the oracles of God; and are become such as have need of milk, and not of strong meat. For everyone that uses milk is unskillful in the word of righteousness: for he is a babe. But strong meat belongeth to them who are of full age; even those who by reason of use have their senses exercised to discern both good and evil.

Here Paul is explaining the importance of growing up in the word of God, saying that those who should have been teaching needed someone to teach them, instead. And that's true today; there are many people in our churches who can't even find the book of Genesis, because they don't spend time reading their Bible. The word of God is the only thing that will feed and nourish your baby.

Now that you know you're pregnant, it is your responsibility to make sure your diet is right. You can't go through life living for yourself; there is something in you that the world needs, and it's your job to nourish it until birth. Can you imagine where the world would be if Mary hadn't taken care of her baby?

Begin praising God now for letting you carry such an awesome baby. Every purpose God gives you is always bigger than you. The baby you are carrying will change the world, so feed it with the only nourishment meant for it, God's word.

CHAPTER FOUR

ULTRASOUND

Ultrasound technology directs high-frequency sounds into the body, where the tissue interfaces reflect the sound, and the resulting pattern is processed by a computer to produce a photograph or moving image on a television screen. Ultrasound can be used to examine many parts of the body, but its best-known application is the examination of the fetus during pregnancy.

The sound waves in an ultrasound beam are inaudible to humans. They are produced by a rapidly oscillating crystal; a device called a transducer transmits the sound waves and receives the echoes. The transducer must be in close contact with the skin, where a jellylike substance is used to improve the transmission of sound.

Unlike an x-ray, an ultrasound is safe during pregnancy, with no risk to either the fetus or the mother. It can tell the parents their child's gender, and it is used to monitor the development and well-being of the fetus, providing information about its age, head size, and estimated due date. If the doctor suspects multiple fetuses, an ultrasound can confirm that suspicion.

With a spiritual pregnancy, as with a physical one, it's exciting to find out exactly what you're carrying. When you have your spiritual ultrasound, God will let you know what He has planned for you. Remember, the ultrasound will provide a picture of what's inside you.

Let's see what God told Habakkuk about this picture or vision:

I will stand upon my watch, and set me upon the tower, and will watch to see what he will say unto

me, and what I shall answer when I am reproved. And the Lord answered me, and said, write the vision, and make it plain upon tables, that he may run that readeth it. For the vision is yet for an appointed time, but at the end it shall speak and not lie: though it tarry, wait for it; because it will surely come, it will not tarry.

Hab. 2:1-3 (King James Bible)

What we're reading about here is Habakkuk's spiritual ultrasound; Habakkuk has gone to God to learn what God has in store for His people. If you want to know what's inside you, do what Habakkuk did: ask the one who put it there. God tells Habakkuk to write down the vision and make it plain, so that he can always look at it and know where he is.

It's a good idea to write down everything that the Lord shows you for your future, just as a doctor will give expectant parents an ultrasound image of their unborn child. This picture gives them a view of three things:

1. **It shows the growth of the child.** This is important to the parents because it lets them know that their baby is growing at the right rate; if so, they know they're doing things correctly. You need to create your spiritual picture so that you can see exactly where you are in the growth process. When you write it down, you can see where you are in the process, and if the baby isn't growing properly, you can make the necessary changes.

2. **It shows the development of the child.** By writing down his vision, Habakkuk had something in hand to show him what it should look like. That way, he would be able to see anything that was not right. By getting an ultrasound picture, the doctor can ensure that a child's heart, head, and limbs are developing properly. A picture can also help you with the development of your spiritual baby. Compare it to where you are and where you need to be, so that you can make sure you're on course.

3. **It shows the well–being of the baby.** It's important to know if God wants you to make any changes. Even if you feel your baby is healthy, you may be having complications. Sometimes you'll think you're on the right track, just to find out you're a little off course. By having a picture, you will stay where you need to be.

My sheep hear my voice, and I know them, and they follow me.

John 10:27 (King James Bible)

Jesus is saying here that if you are part of His flock, you should know His voice. Let's look at this statement for a minute. The word voice means "phone" or "sound." Jesus is saying that you should know what He sounds like—and the only way to know that is to know the word of God, because *He sounds like the Bible, from Genesis to Revelation.*

Consider the word *ultrasound* and its base words, *ultra* and *sound*. Just as a doctor sends sound waves through a woman's body to reflect the life inside her, God will send an ultra (maximum) amount of sound (His word) into you to reflect what's inside you.

And just as a doctor uses a jellylike substance smeared on the skin to detect inaudible sounds and echoes, God uses the Holy Spirit like oil, to send His word through your body. When you have the Spirit inside you, you should echo back what He has said. Without receiving Jesus as your savior and the gift of the Holy Spirit, you can't hear His voice with your ears. The Holy Spirit smeared all over you will enhance your transmission of sound. Let's look at Romans 8:26-30:

> **Likewise the Spirit also helpeth our infirmities: for we know not what we should pray for as we ought: but the Spirit itself maketh intercession for us with groanings which cannot be uttered. And he that searches the heart knoweth what is in the mind of the Spirit, because he maketh intercession for the saints according to the will of God. And we know that all things work together for the good to them that love God, to them who are the called according to his purpose. For whom he did foreknow, he also did predestinate to be conformed to the image of his son, that he might be the firstborn among many brethren. Moreover whom he did predestinate, them he also called: and whom he called them he also justified: and whom he justified them he also glorified.**

Paul wants you to realize that God has your whole future in His hands—that no matter what comes your way, He has already given you the victory. Everything was planned out even before you were born, Paul says. And this is important, because it means that you serve a God who is prepared for everything. That's why you should go to God for your ultrasound and let Him tell you what the future holds for you. His word is powerful enough to reveal everything about you, as it says in Hebrews 4:12:

For the word of God is quick, and powerful, and sharper than any two-edged sword, piercing even to the dividing asunder of soul and spirit, and of the joints and marrow, and is a discerner of the thoughts and intents of the heart.

God uses His word to show you everything that there is to know about you. His word will open you up, bringing you face to face with the real you. You will begin to see things that you didn't realize were there. It's just like an ultrasound—you get to see the inside of you.

Consider God's use of language in Jeremiah 1:4-5:

Then the word of the Lord came unto me, saying, Before I formed thee in the belly I knew thee; and before thou camest forth out of the womb I sanctified thee, and I ordained thee a prophet to the nations.

Here you see God performing an ultrasound on Jeremiah; He tells Jeremiah that He knew him before He placed him in his mother's womb. What an awesome statement to hear from God, that He knew you even before you were born!

God is letting Jeremiah know that his future has already been determined.

That's why you now realize that you're pregnant—because God is getting you ready for the future. He is revealing His plans for your life, plans that were set in place before you were even conceived. I believe that the most exciting time in life is when you realize your purpose for coming into the world.

What is God telling you? What has He showed you about your future? Are you excited about the possibilities? The best thing about the whole process is that the baby you're carrying has been put there by God. And when God fathers a child, no one needs to worry about child support.

Take a moment now to thank God for revealing His plan for your life. Wherever you are, if it's possible, praise Him for thinking enough of you to let you be a part of His divine will.

Let's look at the story of Moses and God's vision for him:

Now Moses kept the flock of Jethro his father in law, the priest of Midian: and he led the flock to the backside of the desert, and came to the mountain of God, even to Horeb. And the angel of the Lord appeared unto him in a flame of fire out of the midst of a bush: and he looked, and, behold, the bush burned with fire, and the bush was not consumed. And Moses said I would now turn aside, and see this great sight, why the bush is not burnt. And when the Lord saw he turned aside to see, God called unto him out of the midst

of the bush, and said, Moses, Moses, and he said, here am I. And he said, draw not nigh hither: put off thy shoes from thy feet, for the place whereon thy standest is Holy ground. Moreover he said, I am the God of thy father, the God of Abraham, the God of Isaac, and the God of Jacob. And Moses hid his face; for he was afraid to look upon God. And the Lord said, I have surely seen the affliction of my people, which are in Egypt, and have heard their cry by reason of their taskmasters; for I know their sorrows; And I am come down to deliver them out of the hands of the Egyptians, and to bring them up out of that land unto a good land and a large, unto a land flowing with milk and honey; unto the place of the Canaanites, and the Hittites, and the Amorites, and the Perizzites, and the Hivites, and the Jebusites. Now therefore, behold, the cry of the children is come unto me: and I have also seen the oppression wherewith the Egyptians oppress them. Come now therefore, and I will send thee unto Pharaoh, that thou mayest bring forth my people the children of Israel out of Egypt. And Moses said unto God, who am I, that I should go unto Pharaoh, and that I should bring forth the children of Israel out of Egypt? And he said, certainly I will be with thee; and this shall be a token unto thee, that I have sent thee: when thou has brought forth the people out of Egypt, ye shall serve God upon this mountain.

Exod. 3:1-12 (King James Bible)

In this story, God calls to Moses from inside the burning bush and tells Moses what He wants him to do: to tell

Pharaoh to let His people go. Of course, Moses had no idea that his life would take such a dramatic turn; he had assumed he would live happily ever after with his new wife. But God has other plans for him, a life plan which He reveals in this ultrasound.

Let's take a closer look at this story for a minute. Moses is keeping his father-in-law's sheep when God calls to him from the bush. Notice that Moses turns aside to see. That's what you have to do—stop and hear what the Lord has to say to you. Sometimes we're so busy we don't make time to listen to the Lord. Notice also that God doesn't even begin to speak until Moses turns to see. Before He begins to speak, the Lord will wait to see if you are listening.

Like Moses, you need to realize that you serve a holy God; coming into His presence will require you to cast aside some things, like the sins in your life. That's what God means when He begins to tell Moses all the things that he must do and how to do them. Remember, the baby that you are carrying will bless a nation, so it's critical that you follow God's plan to the letter. The ultrasound that Moses received was overwhelming to him, so God let him take along his brother Aaron for support.

Remember, if you can accomplish a vision alone, you get the glory. If you can't, God gets the glory. God always gives you things to do that you cannot accomplish on your own; He makes sure that you need Him to accomplish them. I know that the results of your ultrasound may seem overwhelming, but don't worry—that's how you'll know it came from the Lord. Whenever He gives you something to do, He will provide everything you need to accomplish it.

CHAPTER FIVE

ABORTION

Abortion is the termination of pregnancy before birth, resulting in or accompanied by the death of the fetus. Some abortions occur naturally because the fetus hasn't developed normally or because the mother has an injury or disorder that prevents her from carrying the pregnancy to term. This kind of spontaneous abortion is commonly known as a miscarriage. Other abortions are induced, intentionally brought on because the pregnancy is unwanted or presents a risk to the mother's health.

A human pregnancy lasts an average of thirty-nine to forty weeks. That period is divided into three stages, known as trimesters. The first trimester consists of the first thirteen weeks; the second trimester spans weeks fourteen to twenty-four; and the third trimester lasts from the twenty-fifth week to birth. Abortions in the first trimester of pregnancy are easier and safer to perform, while abortions in the second and third trimesters require more complicated procedures and pose a greater risk to the woman's health.

An estimated fifty million abortions are performed worldwide each year. For various reasons, many women feel that they cannot carry their baby to term, and they abort the child. Some don't even believe that what they are carrying is a baby; they think that if they abort the child early enough, they won't be hurting anyone.

I know that there are times when you think about giving up on the plans that the Lord has shown you, but this is not the time to throw in the towel. You have an awesome responsibility to carry a child who will change the world. Hold your course—don't let the devil trick you into aborting your life's mission. God placed that vision in

your heart, and before it reached your heart, it was in His.
As a reminder of that truth, let's review what God told
Jeremiah:

**Before I formed thee in the belly I knew thee;
and before thou camest forth out of the womb I
sanctified thee, and I ordained thee a prophet unto
the nations.**

Jer. 1:5 (King James Bible)

It's not surprising that so many people believe that the
life they are carrying is not life until it reaches a certain
stage—that's a trick of the enemy. The devil has tricked
people all across this country with that lie. When God
says He knew Jeremiah before he was born, that's saying
a lot. It tells me that God predestinates our existence. Just
think, out of 250 million sperm, only one survived to
create you—because God planned it that way. There are no
mistakes in this world. I know you thought you showed up
just because your parents came together one night. Well, I
want you to know that you are not a mistake and you are
not a creation of someone's lust. You were appointed for
just such a time as this, and God has wonderful plans for
you. God had to get Jeremiah to understand this before He
was able to use him.

Let's look at some biblical examples to see what happens
when men try to abort their purpose. We'll begin with the
story of Jonah:

**Now the word of the Lord came unto Jonah the
son of Amittai, saying, Arise, go to Nineveh, that
great city, and cry against it; for their wickedness**

is come up before me. But Jonah rose up to flee unto Tarshish from the presence of the Lord, and went down to Joppa; and he found a ship going to Tarshish: so he paid the fare thereof, and went down into it, to go with them unto Tarshish from the presence of the Lord. But the Lord sent out a great wind into the sea, and there was a mighty tempest in the sea, so that ship was like to be broken. Then the mariners were afraid, and cried every man unto his god, and cast forth the wares that were in the ship into the sea, to lighten it of them, but Jonah was gone down into the sides of the ship; and he lay, and was fast asleep. So the shipmaster came to him, and said unto him, what meanest thou, o sleeper? Arise, call upon thy God, if so be that God will think upon us, that we perish not. And they said everyone to his fellow, come, and let us cast lots, that we may know for who causes this evil is upon us. So they cast lots, and the lot fell upon Jonah. Then said they unto him, tell us, we pray thee, for who causes this evil is upon us; what is thy occupation? And whence comest thou? What is thy country? And of what people are thy? And he said unto them, I am a Hebrew; and I fear the Lord, the God of heaven, which has made the sea and dry land. Then were the men exceedingly afraid, and said unto him, why has thou done this? For the men knew that he fled from the presence of the Lord, because he had told them. Then said they unto him, what shall we do unto thee, that the sea may be calm unto us? For the sea wrought, and was tempestuous. And he said unto them, take me up, and cast me forth into the sea; so shall the sea be calm unto you:

for I know that for my sake this great tempest is upon you. Nevertheless the men rowed hard to bring it to the land; but they could not; for the sea wrought, and was tempestuous against them. Wherefore they cried unto the Lord, and said, we beseech thee, o Lord, we beseech thee, let us not perish for this man's life, and lay not unto us innocent blood: for thou, o Lord, hast done as it pleased thee. So they took up Jonah, and cast him forth into the sea: and the sea ceased from her raging. Then the men feared the Lord exceedingly, and offered a sacrifice unto the Lord, and made vows. Now the Lord had made a great fish to swallow up Jonah. And Jonah was in the belly of the fish three days and three nights.

Jonah 1:1-17 (King James Bible)

THE PREGNANCY

God gave Jonah clear instructions to go to Nineveh and preach to the people there. This was Jonah's baby. God created him for this very purpose, to bring a message to the people; He impregnated Jonah with this purpose, to cry against a city in need of repentance.

Sometimes God gives you tasks that don't seem very important. But if God takes the time to send you on a mission, it is a great work. There are people who are depending on your faithfulness to God. What is it that the Lord has asked you to do? What's on the inside of you that needs to get out?

THE ABORTION

God gave Jonah a simple task: to preach to the people of Nineveh. But Jonah didn't want to go; some theologians say that's because the people there were of a different race. Regardless of the reason, instead of doing what the Lord asked him to do, Jonah decided to abort God's purpose and do his own thing. According to the Bible, he headed in the opposite direction, to Tarshish. He thought that by getting on a boat and running from the Lord, he would get away. But he soon found out that you can't run from God.

CONSEQUENCES OF ABORTION

Jonah learned that when you abort your purpose, there are consequences. He got on the ship and headed away from Nineveh with nothing on his mind but rest; after boarding, he went down to the side of the ship and fell asleep. He thought everything was fine. But the Lord caused the sea to rock and the winds to blow against the ship that was carrying Jonah. The men on the ship didn't know what was going on. They began to call on their gods, but nothing happened, so they decided to wake Jonah up. Because of his disobedience, the whole ship was in danger, and when the other men realized that he was the problem, they threw him overboard. The Lord had a great fish waiting for him in the water, and the fish swallowed him. Jonah stayed in the fish's belly for three days.

Whenever you abort your purpose there will be consequences, and they will affect more people than just you. Notice that when Jonah disobeyed God, it affected everyone on the ship. That's what happens when you disobey God: everyone around you suffers.

When a woman has an abortion, she likely thinks that the crisis is all over. But just think—because of that abortion, someone the world needed will never arrive. That child could have been someone's dad, mother, sister, brother, uncle, aunt, or pastor, but because his or her mother had an abortion, the world will never know that person. What if that child had grown up to discover a cure for cancer or AIDS?

That's why it is vital that you stay your course and not abort God's plans for your life. Someone is waiting for an answer to their problems, and that answer could be inside of you.

Of course, the people around Jonah weren't the only ones who suffered; Jonah did, too. According to the Bible, God created a great fish to swallow Jonah, who stayed in the fish's belly until he was ready to do what he was commanded to do. Finally Jonah repented and ran to Nineveh, so thankful for the second chance that he made the three-day journey in just one day.

Luke 9:62 reveals what God thinks about us aborting His plans for our lives:

And Jesus said unto him, no man, having put his hand to the plough, and looking back, is fit for the kingdom of God.

Jesus tells us that if we look back—if we abort our mission—we are not fit for the kingdom of God. So make sure that you consider the cost of quitting before you take on your responsibility.

We can learn about this further in this story of the
disciples:

> Simon Peter said unto them, I go a fishing. They
> said unto him, we also go with thee. They went
> forth, and entered into a ship immediately; and that
> night they caught nothing. But when the morning
> was now come, Jesus stood on the shore: but the
> disciples knew not that it was Jesus. Then Jesus
> said unto them, children have ye any meat? They
> answered him, no. And he said unto them, cast the
> net on the right side of the ship, and ye shall find.
> They cast therefore, and now they were not able
> to draw it for the multitude of fish. Therefore that
> disciple whom Jesus loved said unto Peter, it is the
> Lord. Now when Simon Peter heard that it was the
> Lord, he girt his fisher's coat unto him, (for he was
> naked) and did cast himself into the sea. And the
> other disciples came in a little ship; (for they were
> not far from the land, but as it were two hundred
> cubits,) dragging the net with fishes. As soon then
> as they were come to land, they saw a fire of coals
> there, and fish laid thereon, and bread. Jesus said
> unto them, bring of the fish, which ye have now
> caught. Simon Peter went up, and drew the net to
> land, full of great fishes, a hundred and fifty and
> three: and for all there were so many, yet was not
> the net broken. Jesus said unto them, come and
> dine. And none of the disciples durst ask him,
> who art thou? Knowing that it was the Lord. Jesus
> then cometh, and taketh bread, and giveth them,
> and fish likewise. This is now the third time that
> Jesus showed himself to his disciples, after that he
> was risen from the dead. So when they had dined,

Jesus said to Simon Peter, Simon, son of Jonas, loves thou me more than these? He said unto him, yes, Lord; thou know that I love thee. He said unto him, feed my lambs. He said to him again the second time, Simon, son of Jonas, loves thou me? He said unto him, yea, Lord; thou know that I love thee. He said unto him, feed my sheep. He said unto him the third time, Simon, son of Jonas, loves thou me? And he said unto him, Lord, thou know all things; thou know that I love thee. Jesus said unto him, feed my sheep.

John 21:3-17 (King James Bible)

After Jesus's death, the disciples went back to what they were doing before He had called them: they went fishing. In other words, Peter and the other disciples were about to have an abortion; they were afraid of what was happening, so they reverted back to what they were used to doing. The problem was that they didn't catch anything. Isn't it true that whenever you go back to your old life, it's never the way it used to be? When you are spiritually pregnant, a change has taken place inside you, and you won't find enjoyment or even success in your old lifestyle. The disciples are a good example. They didn't catch a thing all night.

After they had been fishing all night, Jesus asked them what they had to show for their efforts. The answer, of course, was nothing. Whenever you find yourself at odds with God's will, you won't have anything to show for your human efforts. There is no real success outside the scope of God's will.

I want you to notice something here: Jesus already had what they were looking for. The Bible says that when the disciples got to shore, Jesus already had fish and bread. Not only did He have what they were looking for, but He also told them how to get all the fish they needed—and more—by casting their net on the other side of the ship.

Like the disciples, you are nothing without God and His plans for your life. Whenever He chooses a task for you, you should find fulfillment in nothing but what He has asked you to do.

Sometimes you'll feel that the task at hand is too hard and not worth the pain you're going through, that it would be easier to give up. But don't abort—Jesus is right there with you, and He promises never to leave or forsake you. He is the only one you need to make it. Whenever you feel like giving up, just ask Him for some strength to make it through, and He will help you. According to the Bible, this fishing incident was the third time that the risen Jesus showed Himself to the disciples. This shows you that the Lord will be there whenever you need Him.

Notice also in this story that Jesus asks Peter the same question three times: Do you love Me? And all three times, Peter answers yes. Jesus wants Peter to understand that He still loves him, no matter how many times Peter denied Him earlier. Isn't it wonderful to know that your God loves you unconditionally? And by asking this question, Jesus also is redirecting Peter back to the disciples' true mission. They were chosen to go fishing for souls, not fish.

Sometimes God's plan is so important that He won't let you abort; He loves you too much to let you go. He's telling you that even though you've entertained thoughts of aborting His plan, He still loves you and wants you to be a part of His divine will. Take a moment right now to praise Him for his tender mercy and loving kindness.

Don't let the devil whisper in your ear and tell you something different than what the Lord has said; he will always try to get you to abort your purpose. He will also take scriptures out of context to get you to believe a lie. Ever since the devil had his own spiritual abortion, it has been his plan to perform the same operation on anyone he can. He did it to Adam and Eve, Cain, Lot's wife, the people of Noah's day, and a third of the angels in heaven. He even tried to get Jesus to have a spiritual abortion in the wilderness.

WHAT IF

What if Eve had had an abortion? We wouldn't have Cain, Able, and Seth.

What if Noah's wife had had an abortion? We wouldn't have Shem, Ham, and Japheth.

What if Terah's wife had had an abortion? We wouldn't have Abraham.

What if Sarah had had an abortion? We wouldn't have Isaac.

What if Rebekah had had an abortion? We wouldn't have Esau and Jacob.

What if Rachel had had an abortion? We wouldn't have Joseph and Benjamin.

What if the daughter of Levi had had an abortion? We wouldn't have Moses.

What if Nun's wife had had an abortion? We wouldn't have Joshua.

What if Hannah had had an abortion? We wouldn't have Samuel.

What if Jesse's wife had had an abortion? We wouldn't have David.

What if David's wife had had an abortion? We wouldn't have Solomon.

What if Paul's or Peter's mother had had an abortion?

What if Mary had had an abortion? My God! We wouldn't have our Lord and Savior, Jesus Christ.

And what if *your* mother had had an abortion? You would not be reading this book, and the world would be without a beautiful person.

The same thing is true in the spiritual sense: you cannot abort the plans God has for your life, because someone is waiting on what's inside you. The graveyard is full of unfulfilled destinies. There are authors who never wrote a book, entrepreneurs who never opened a business, preachers who never gave a sermon, teachers who never taught a class, dancers who never danced, cooks who never cooked, producers who never made a record, singers who never sang a song—people with all kinds of skills whom the world has been deprived of. Don't add to the riches of the graveyard. Give your baby to the world.

CHAPTER SIX

FIRST TRIMESTER

Most pregnancies last thirty-nine to forty weeks, a period divided into three stages known as trimesters. The first trimester consists of the first thirteen weeks, the second trimester spans weeks fourteen to twenty-four, and the third trimester lasts from the twenty-fifth week until birth.

The first few months of pregnancy are the most critical for the developing infant, because during this period the infant's brain, limbs, and internal organs are formed. For this reason, a pregnant woman should be especially careful about taking any kind of medication except on the advice of a physician who knows that she is pregnant. And of course, she should avoid smoking and drinking.

THE IMPORTANCE OF TIME

The lifestyle choices a woman makes during the first trimester of her pregnancy largely determine how well the pregnancy will go. What she eats and drinks and her activities will directly affect the baby. Those first thirteen weeks are crucial to the baby's health, and to hers.

If the pregnancy goes well, it will last about forty weeks—a significant point, as the number forty is a very important one in the Bible. Every time a biblical figure is tested or goes through some sort of trial, it lasts forty days. Consider this story from Genesis:

> **For yet seven days, and I will cause it to rain upon the earth forty days and forty nights; and every living substance that I have made will I destroy from off the face of the earth. And Noah did according to**

all that the Lord commanded him. And Noah was six hundred years old when the flood of water was upon the earth. And Noah went in, and his sons, and his wife, and his son's wives with him, into the ark, because of the waters of the flood.

Of clean beasts, and of beasts that are not clean, and of fowls, and of everything that creepeth upon the earth, There went in two and two unto Noah into the ark, the male and the female, as God had commanded Noah. And it came to pass after seven days, that the waters of the flood were upon the earth. In the six hundredth year of Noah's life, in the second month, the seventeenth day of the month, the same day were all the fountains of the great deep broken up, and the windows of heaven were opened. And the rain was upon the earth forty days and forty nights.

Gen. 7:4-12 (King James Bible)

Because of the sins of the people, God destroyed the world by flood. He caused it to rain for forty days and forty nights, using that number to purify the earth. I believe that the first stage of that flood was crucial. Can you imagine what Noah's family went through on the boat when it first began to rain? They had to listen helplessly as all their friends begged to be let in.

The first trimester of pregnancy—physical or spiritual—is always difficult, but you have to get through that first stage before you can move on to the next. The baby inside of you will take time to develop. Consider the children of Israel, who had to wait forty days for Moses to bring them the law:

And Moses went up into the mount, and a cloud covered the mount. And the glory of the Lord abode upon Mount Sinai, and the clouds covered it six days: and the seventh day he called unto Moses out of the midst of the cloud. And the sight of the glory of the Lord was like devouring fire on the top of the mount in the eyes of the children of Israel. And Moses went into the midst of the cloud, and gat him up into the mount: and Moses was in the mount forty days and forty nights.

Exod. 24:15-18 (King James Bible)

After God brought the children of Israel out of Egypt, He took them into the wilderness to give them His laws. Notice the significant number: it took Moses forty days and forty nights to come down from Mount Sinai with the laws.

Now let's look at the test of Jesus in the desert:

Then was Jesus led up of the Spirit into the wilderness to be tempted of the devil. And when he was fasted forty days and forty nights, he was afterward hungry.

Matt. 4:1-2 (King James Bible)

Jesus was led into the wilderness by the Holy Spirit, who brought Him there to be tempted by the devil. God never tempts you; He only tests you. The word *tempted* is used because that is what the devil does. Temptation is designed to make you sin, but testing is meant to show you exactly where you are. When a teacher gives you a test, she is not trying to fail you; she's trying to see what you have learned and what you need to learn. The same is true with God. He is not trying to destroy you; He is improving you.

> **Let no man say when he is tempted, I am tempted of God: for God cannot be tempted with evil, neither tempted he any man.**
>
> **James 1:13 (King James Bible)**

Notice that the temptation of Jesus happened directly after His baptism, during the first stage of His public ministry. Before God could put the world in His hands, Jesus had to be tested. According to the Bible, Jesus fasted forty days and forty nights. This was the period before the test, the purifying stage.

This is the same thing that you will have to go through in the first stage of your pregnancy. This is a time that has been set aside for you and God to become closer. The first stage of pregnancy is beautiful; you begin to notice all the changes that are taking place inside you. I believe that the first stage of Jesus's forty days and forty nights was important, because what He did at the beginning of his time in the desert would reflect on the entire period.

> **To whom also he showed himself alive after his passion by many infallible proofs, being seen of them forty days, and speaking of the things pertaining to the kingdom of God.**
>
> **Acts 1:3 (King James Bible)**

Jesus not only was tested for forty days and forty nights, but He also showed himself to His followers for forty days after His resurrection.

It is important to understand that spiritual pregnancy is a process you must go through to get where you need to be. This first stage is a critical part of that process. And just as one woman's pregnancy might last longer than another's, this stage involves no set time span; yours might be different from someone else's, depending on God's will and how you handle yourself. With a spiritual pregnancy, what you have inside you will materialize based upon your growth.

THE DEVELOPMENT

During the first, crucial stage of pregnancy, the child is starting to develop. How it develops is based on how well the mother takes care of her body, as monitored through regular checkups. She needs to visit her physician regularly to ensure that her child is growing at a normal rate. During her checkups, the doctor will be looking at several things that will be critical to the child's survival in this world. Let's examine these four areas:

1. THE BRAIN (MIND)

During a prenatal ultrasound, the size of the fetus's head is measured to estimate its age. In general, the bigger the head, the older the child, unless it is suffering from some disease. The head needs to continue to grow so that the fetus can develop. If the head isn't growing, the brain isn't developing—which means there's something wrong with the whole body.

The same thing is true with the spirit. In order to mature in the ways of God, you must increase your knowledge of Him. You can tell where you are in this process by taking measure of your mind (head). Is your mind developing, or is there something wrong?

Your mind is the seat of your intellect, the place where the spirit speaks to you. When the Bible says that God speaks to your heart, it's really referring to your mind—that is, God speaks to the part of you that makes you different from animals. Your mind controls your whole body, giving your body orders to carry out. That's why it is so important that you develop your mind. The mind is so critical that if part of the brain shuts down, the body will be paralyzed.

Proverbs 4:5-9 encourages us to get Godly wisdom and understanding:

> **Get wisdom, get understanding: forget it not; neither decline from the words of my mouth. Forsake her not, and she shall preserve thee: love her, and she shall keep thee. Wisdom is the principal thing; therefore get wisdom: and with all thy getting get understanding. Exalt her, and she shall promote thee: she shall bring thee to honor, when thou dost embrace her. She shall give to thine head an ornament of grace: a crown of glory shall she deliver to thee.**

You are instructed here to get the wisdom and understanding that you need for a successful life—and this wisdom and understanding must come from God Himself. According to James 1:5, God says we should come to Him for wisdom:

If any of you lack wisdom, let him ask of God, that giveth to all men liberally, and upbraideth not; and it shall be given him.

Wisdom is knowing how; understanding is knowing when. And gaining wisdom and understanding is the only way to ensure the development of the mind. Remember that it's not what you put *on* your head that matters, but what you put *in* your head. Too many people go around trying to look intelligent, but the truth is obvious the moment they open their mouths.

Just as the umbilical cord sends nourishment from mother to baby, God's word will send wisdom and understanding to your mind for your nourishment and growth.

In order for us to make the necessary changes to our thought process, God encourages us to renew our minds. Let's look at Romans 12:1-2:

I beseech you therefore, brethren, by the mercies of God, that you present your bodies a living sacrifice, holy, acceptable unto God, which is your reasonable service. And be not conformed to this world: but be ye transformed by the renewing of your mind, that ye may prove what is that good, and perfect, will of God.

Remember, the body gets its orders from the head (mind), and if the head is messed up, then the body will be, too. This is why spiritual pregnancy requires a mind change. You cannot have the mind telling the feet to talk and the hands to walk, or the eyes to hear and the ears to see. This is what the devil will do to your mind if God doesn't have it; he will have you all twisted. That's why Paul tells us here to give our body and mind to God. If your baby is going to develop, it will need the right kind of mind—a Christ-like mind.

If we are going to develop a mind like Christ's, we must have a mental washing and a reprogramming of old mindsets. Since it is critical that we renew our minds in order to succeed in His purpose, let's take a look at how the renewal process works.

The mind is the seat of reflective consciousness and understanding, the place where all our thoughts are housed. God gave us this very powerful tool to help us function in the world. We can go only as far as our mind will take us; that's why it is very important that we develop it. Notice that in Romans 12:2, Paul says not to conform to this world, but to be transformed by the renewal of the mind. Key here is the word *transform*—that is, to change into another form, to change in character and conduct.

Let's look at what Paul says to the Corinthian church about this kind of mind renewal:

Now the Lord is the Spirit, and where the Spirit of the Lord is, there is liberty (emancipation from

bondage, freedom). And all of us, as with unveiled face, [*because we*] continued to behold [*in the Word of God*] as in a mirror the glory of the Lord, are constantly being transfigured into His very own image in ever increasing splendor and from one degree of glory to another; [*for this comes*] from the Lord [*Who is*] the Spirit.

2 Cor. 3:17-18 (The Amplified Bible)

In this text, Paul is trying to explain to the Corinthians that all real mind renewal come through the spirit of God. It is accomplished by reading His word while reflecting on our lives, and by realizing that we are not perfect, but that by allowing His word to wash us, we can become just like Christ. In the process, Paul says, we are transfigured into God's own image.

I want you to notice that this change takes place in your soul. In the first chapter I touched on the fact that we are made of three parts: body, soul, and spirit. This is important, because your mind is, of course, housed in your body, the soulless part of you. But God is not trying to change your body; He is concerned about your soul, the part of you that controls your whole body. If you change your mind, therefore, you will change your life.

A MENTAL CLEANSING

It is important that you cleanse your mind of any old, nonproductive mindset that keeps you from God's best purposes. This is critical, because your mind is a powerful tool, and it can either help or hurt you. Let's consider some important facts about our thought process:

1. Our conscious mind organizes facts, but our subconscious mind shapes opinions, and these opinions affect how the conscious mind does its work.
2. Our subconscious mind stores information through our senses, whether that information is factual or not. We base our actions on all the things we have seen and heard.
3. Our decisions are based on information that enters into our thinking subliminally.

Now you can see why it is important that you renew your mind. It would be impossible to accomplish anything worth doing in life with a mind that's stuck in old ways of thinking. For a successful spiritual pregnancy, it is important that you develop your mind in a deliberate way; don't allow just anything to enter your mind.

Notice my third point—that information can subliminally enter your mind. This happens through your senses of taste, touch, smell, hear, and sight. When a company wants to sell you something, they'll appeal to one of your senses to get the message across. They know that if they can get you to internalize their message, they can sell you anything.

The subconscious mind is like a warehouse, storing all the information you've put there through reading and listening. This is why you can multitask—walking and reading a book at the same time, for example—because your subconscious mind already knows what to do. It is this subconscious mind that you must wash of all ungodly and unproductive things.

Look at what God tells Jerusalem in Jer. 4:14:

O Jerusalem, wash your heart from wickedness, that you may be saved! How long shall your iniquitous and grossly offensive thoughts lodge within you?

God tells the people of Jerusalem that it's their job to wash the offensive thoughts that are lodged within them. Where are the thoughts lodged? I believe they are in the subconscious.

Let's look at the book of Hebrews to see how the blood of Jesus can cleanse our thoughts:

How much more surely shall the blood of Christ, Who by virtue of [*His*] eternal Spirit [*His own preexistent divine personality*] has offered Himself as an unblemished sacrifice to God, purify our consciences from dead works and lifeless observances to serve the [*ever*] living God?

Heb. 9:14 (The Amplified Bible)

How much information is stored in your mind depends on your age. If the information does not line up with God's word, then the Blood of Christ is powerful enough to wash it away.

Once the mind has been washed by the word of God, you must replace the old information with new information. This is the part I call a mental reprogramming.

A MENTAL REPROGRAMMING

This part of the process is important because your mind is the control center, so you must be very careful about what you allow to pass through it. You must program it with information that will help you accomplish God's plan. There are several points about this stage that I want you to remember:

1. You must meditate on His word.
2. You must guard your senses against everything ungodly.
3. You must accept God's word as the final authority in your life.
4. You must bring your every thought into line with His word.

Reprogramming old mindsets is not an easy process, but it is necessary. By meditating on God's word, you will force your mind to submit to a new way of thinking. It is His word that has the power to change your mind.

In Philippians 2:5, Paul tells the church at Philippi to have the same mind as Christ:

Let this mind be in you, which was also in Christ Jesus.

It is the spiritual part of you that needs to receive God's instruction. Remember, if you are going to be spiritually pregnant, you will need to allow His word to speak to your spirit. Jesus allowed the Spirit of God to lead and minister to Him. Make the decision to accept God's word as the final authority in your life. Let His word rest in your mind.

Remember: *the body will go only where the mind takes it.*

2. THE ARMS

The arms are the part of the baby that will perform the physical work, so they need to be strong and healthy. During prenatal visits, the doctor will check to make sure the baby has two developing arms. If the baby does not, it will affect how he is viewed in the world and what he will be able to do.

Because of this, the arms are as important as the mind. You need wisdom and knowledge to be successful, but you also need hands to work your future.

Let's look at Proverbs 31:17-20, which describes the virtuous woman:

She girdeth her loins with strength, and strengtheneth her arms. She proceeds that her merchandise is good: her candle goeth not out by night. She layeth her hands to the spindle, and her hands hold the distaff. She stretched out her hand to the poor; yea, she reached forth her hands to the needy.

Notice the emphasis on physical work here—the virtuous woman strengthens her arms and works with her hands. In a spiritual sense, too, you must make sure that your arms and hands are developing, for they are tools God has given you to perform your tasks. Whatever your hands are busy doing will build your future. Therefore it is important that your baby's arms are developing well, because underdeveloped arms will lead to underdeveloped work. The stronger your arms and hands, the more you will be able to do.

Notice all the things this virtuous woman is capable of once she strengthens her arms and hands. She can lay her hands to the spindle, hold the distaff, and stretch it to the poor and needy. What are you doing with your arms and hands right now? What in your life is getting most of your time and energy?

When a man first begins to lift weights, he can't start off with heavy ones; he must start with lighter weights and work his way up, as his muscles get used to the heavier burden. In the same way, God cannot give you a lot to do until you've developed the capacity to handle it. The stronger your arms and hands, the more you can handle.

A good example of this truth is found in the story of Simeon, a man who wanted to see the deliverance of Israel:

> **And, behold, there was a man in Jerusalem, whom name was Simeon; and the same man was just and devout, waiting for the consolation of Israel: and the Holy Ghost was upon him. And it was revealed unto him by the Holy Ghost, that he should not see death, before he had seen the Lord Christ. And he came by the Spirit into the temple: and when the parents brought in the child Jesus, to do for him after the customs of the law, Then took he**

**him up in his arms, and blessed God, and said,
Lord, now lettest thou thy servant depart in peace,
according to thy word: For mine eyes have seen
thy salvation.**

Luke 2:25-30 (King James Bible)

All Simeon wanted before he died was to look upon
the savior of the world. According to the Bible, he was
a just and devout man who lived his life for the Lord.
Because Simeon had lived a good life for God, the Lord
took it one step further: He allowed Simeon to hold Jesus. I
believe that if Simeon hadn't been just and devout, the Lord
wouldn't have granted him this wish. But Simeon's arms
were strong; they were prepared for this day. Because he
had developed his arms, he was ready for that moment.

In order to be ready for what the Lord has for you,
you'll have to develop your arms. Remember, God won't
give you more than you can handle. Can you imagine
holding Jesus in your arms? Think about that fact: Simeon
held in his hands the savior of the world. This tells us that
God doesn't trust just anyone with his purpose. Similarly,
a mother doesn't let just anyone hold her child; she is very
particular about who will get that opportunity.

After all the pain a mother has to endure during
childbirth, it is a blessing when the nurse finally lays that
child in her arms—all the pain and heartache is forgotten
the moment the child is placed into her arms. This is the
same feeling I believe Simeon experienced. When Jesus
was placed into his arms, it made all the ups and downs of
life worth it.

If you develop your arms and hands, God will put something in them that will make everything you go through worth the pain.

Psalms 24:3-4 tells us to prepare for God's purpose by having clean hands:

> **Who shall ascend into the hills of the Lord? Or who shall stand in his Holy place? He that hath clean hands, and a pure heart; which hath not lifted up his soul unto vanity, nor sworn deceitfully.**

3. THE LEGS

If a baby is going to learn to walk, his legs will have to develop. Legs get you where you need to go. God created humans with two legs for freedom of mobility. He wanted us to have a way of getting from point A to point B without needing someone to carry us. This is not to say that not having legs is a curse; there are various reasons why people are born without mobility. In general, though, if God had wanted us to crawl, He wouldn't have given us legs.

A newborn baby can't walk. In the beginning, all a child does is lean on his parents for everything. Everywhere he goes he must be carried, until the strength in his legs is developed. It takes time for a baby's legs to become strong enough for him to walk.

The same thing is true with the spirit. You need to develop your legs—that is, your faith. It is what will get you where you need to go.

This is the stage when you need to develop your spiritual legs. You need to make sure that they are getting strong enough to allow you to walk. So let the doctor look at them and tell you how they are developing.

Notice what Paul says in 1 Corinthians 2:5

That your faith should not stand in the wisdom of man, but in the power of God.

If you are going to stand, it will have to be through God's power, not yours. When God gave you faith, He gave you the power to use His word, and that word will hold you up against anything. In Romans 12:3, Paul says God has given us a measure of faith:

For I say, through the grace given unto me, to every man that is among you, not to think of himself more highly than he ought to think; but to think soberly, according as God has dealt to every man the measure of faith.

Developing that faith will strengthen your legs. Remember, strong faith means strong legs; weak faith means weak legs.

For we walk by faith, not by sight.

2 Cor. 5:7 (King James Bible)

In order for you to get somewhere in life, you will have to trust God. And you will not be able to trust God without faith.

Now faith is the substance of things hoped for, the evidence of things not seen.

Heb. 11:1 (King James Bible)

The development of your spiritual legs is crucial, because it represents your ability to move. Physically, legs get you where you want to go. Spiritually, faith gets you where you want to go. In Exodus 14:13, Moses calls on the power of faith when he tells his people to stand still and see the salvation of the Lord:

And Moses said unto the people, fear ye not, stand still, and see the salvation of the Lord, which he will show to you today: for the Egyptians whom ye have seen today, ye shall see them again no more forever.

After the Lord delivered the children of Israel out of Egypt, the Egyptians decided to come after them, trapping the Israelites at the Red Sea. Mountains and water surrounded them, and the Egyptian army was coming up quickly behind them. Notice what happened next: Moses told the Israelites to stand still and see the salvation of the Lord. So they had to stand there and wait on the Lord. Physically, they were supported by their legs. But the only thing that will hold you up in difficult times is faith. Moses had faith, and I believe a few others did, too, but the rest didn't. Spiritual legs took the faithful where physical legs couldn't. The Lord parted the Red Sea, and they crossed over on dry land.

We can see the biblical significance of the legs in John 19:31-36:

The Jews therefore, because it was the preparation, that the body should not remain upon the cross on the Sabbath day (for that Sabbath day was a high day), besought Pilate that their legs might be broken, and that they might be taken away. Then came the soldiers and broke the legs of the first, and of the other, which was crucified with him. But when they came to Jesus, and saw that he was dead already, they broke not his legs: But one of the soldiers with a spear pierced his side, and forthwith came there out blood and water. And he that saw it bare record, and his record is true: and he knoweth that he said true, that ye might believe. For these things were done, that the scriptures should be fulfilled, a bone of him shall not be broken.

BROKEN LEGS

In Jesus's time, it was customary to break the legs of a crucified person to hurry his death. When the Roman soldiers crucified someone, they would nail him to a cross set outside the town walls so the people could see and mock him. Because he was nailed through his hands and feet, he would have to stand up on his legs to catch his breath. After a long time on the cross, this became harder to do, and the crucified person would eventually die. Because it was approaching the Sabbath when Jesus and the two criminals were crucified on Calvary, the soldiers planned to break their legs to hurry their deaths. But when the soldiers came to Jesus, He was already dead, so they did not break a bone in His body.

This is an important fact, because the Bible says that not a bone in His body would be broken, and God made sure that the soldiers didn't break His bones. Jesus had said that no one would take His life—that He would give it willingly. God was in full control of what took place; He gave His son for the world, and no one was able to kill Him. Not only was scripture fulfilled, therefore, but Jesus didn't allow anyone to alter God's plan. He carried it out, just as God intended Him to. He did not let anyone break His walk with the Lord.

This is an important example for you, because you cannot let anyone break your walk—which is exactly what the devil will try to do. He will try to break you down and stop God's plans for your life.

If the soldiers had broken Jesus's legs, they could have claimed to have killed Him. That's why God set the terms of how Jesus would die. Even though the soldiers crucified Jesus, they were not in control—God was. His plans were laid out in Isaiah 53. Jesus had to go past the cross to the grave and back to heaven, where He is still doing work on your behalf. This is why His legs weren't broken. That fact symbolizes that the devil did not break Him or stop His work from going forward.

God has laid out the plans for your life, too. The only one who can stop you is you. So this is when you must make sure that your legs are developing and that nothing is breaking your walk. What is it that keeps you down and depressed? What makes you want to quit? What has you at the point of throwing in the towel? These are things that the devil will send your way to break your walk. He will use anything and anyone he can to stop you from fulfilling your destiny. Don't allow your legs to be broken. Keep your hand in Jesus's hand, and keep moving.

He keepeth all his bones: not one of them is broken.

Psalms 34:20 (King James Bible)

4. THE INTERNAL ORGANS

A baby cannot live without internal organs—the heart, veins, arteries, and so on. During prenatal checkups, the doctor will make sure that these organs are developing and functioning correctly.

In the spiritual sense, also, you need to make sure that these organs are developing. You need to be sure that your heart and arteries—that is, your moral character and holy lifestyle—are working properly. This is the point at which you need to make sure that your life is in order.

HEART (MORAL CHARACTER)

Either make the tree good, and his fruit good; or else make the tree corrupt, and his fruit corrupt: for the tree is known by his fruit. O generation of vipers, how can ye, being evil, speak good things? For out of the abundance of the heart the mouth speaketh. A good man out of the good treasure of the heart bringeth forth good things: and an evil man out of the evil treasure bringeth forth evil things.

Matt. 12:33-35 (King James Bible)

In this passage, Jesus is saying that the heart is the tree and life is the fruit. You can tell what is in a man's heart, He says, by looking at his lifestyle. Whatever comes out of your mouth was already in your heart. That's why you need to develop your heart—because your words will shape your future. If you have evil in your heart, it will come out of your mouth and alter your future.

Remember what God says in Proverbs 18:21:

Death and life are in the power of the tongue: and they that love it shall eat the fruit thereof.

At this stage, you need to make sure there isn't anything in your heart that might come out of your mouth and change your course. To make sure you have a clean heart, read God's word. It will show you what's in your heart.

For the word of God is quick, and powerful, and sharper than any two-edged sword, piercing even to the dividing asunder of soul and spirit, and of the joints and marrow, and is a discerner of the thoughts and intents of the heart.

Heb. 4:12 (King James Bible)

There is nothing that you think that God doesn't already know about you. He knows every thought and intent of your mind. That is why He is the only one who can make you clean.

The heart is the organ that pumps blood to the rest of the body. That's why your heart needs to be right—because your life depends on it. The same thing is true in the spiritual sense: your life depends on what comes from your heart. To whom does your heart belong? Whom do you love with your whole heart? Whomever you love the most, you will try to please the most. Your personality is what other people see, but your character is what God knows. Your personality is who people think you are, but your character is who God knows you are. Your personality is how you act outside, but your character is how you act inside. The two need to merge and become one.

Look at what Jesus says about the heart in Mark 12:29-31:

And Jesus answered him, the first of all the commandments is, hear, o Israel; the Lord our God is one Lord: And thou shalt love the Lord thy God with all thy heart, and with all thy soul, and with all thy mind, and with all thy strength: this is the first commandment. And the second is like, namely this; thou shalt love thy neighbor as thyself. There are no other commandments greater than these.

Here Jesus is giving the order of priorities for your heart. You should love God first, and then you will be able to love your neighbor. Your heart will never be right until you give it to Him first, because He can show you how to love one another. Once this happens, your character will begin to improve. The development of the heart, therefore, is crucial to your growth. Take a moment to check your heart and see where you are in your love walk toward God and your neighbor.

ARTERIES (HOLY LIVING)

Just as the heart pumps blood to the rest of the body, the arteries take that blood and carry it all over the body. If your heart is your character, then your arteries are your lifestyle, the life you have created out of the abundance of your heart. If your heart is right, your life must reflect that; you must live the life you talk about. Barry White put it best when he sang, "You must practice what you preach." Your life must be a walking Bible, because it may be the only Bible some people will read.

Because it is written, be ye holy; for I am holy.

1 Pet. 1:16 (King James Bible)

If there is no clog in your arteries, what's in your heart should come out in your life. Just as the fruit tells what the tree is, the life represents what's in the heart, because the arteries will carry from the heart what it produces.

Here Peter tells Christians that their actions should reflect their status as holy people:

But ye are a chosen generation, a royal priesthood, a holy nation, a peculiar people; that ye should show forth the praises of him who hath called you out of darkness into his marvelous light.

1 Pet. 2:9(King James Bible)

Your internal organs—your heart and arteries—represent everything inside you. Spiritually, they are who you are, everything that there is about you. And just as these organs are important for life, living a holy life is important to your future.

FIRST TRIMESTER BLEEDING

Most couples expect to get pregnant at some point, and when they do, it suddenly dawns on them what a gamble pregnancy actually is. About 15 percent of all pregnancies end in miscarriage, most occurring between the fourth and twelfth weeks of pregnancy. One of the most frightening complications of pregnancy—and one of the most common symptoms to send a woman to her obstetrician—is bleeding in the first trimester. The bad news is that such bleeding is considered abnormal. But the good news is that, most of the time, it's caused by something harmless.

One rare but life-threatening complication often accompanied by bleeding is ectopic pregnancy, in which the fertilized egg implants outside the uterus, either in the abdomen or in a fallopian tube. Other symptoms include sudden, intense pain in the lower abdomen during the seventh or eighth week of pregnancy. If not properly treated by surgical means, an ectopic pregnancy can result in massive internal bleeding and even death. A physician should be contacted immediately if a pregnant women experiences severe abdominal cramping or vaginal bleeding.

Spiritual "bleeding" means that some things are not right in your life, that there are sins in your life that need to be addressed. You need to check with Dr. Jesus to find out what's wrong. This is the time to develop a strong prayer life. You need to stay in touch with the Lord, the only one who can stop the bleeding. Just as a pregnant woman checks with her doctor if she bleeds during her first trimester, you must check with the Lord about your bleeding; He can tell you whether or not He is cleaning you. He is the only one qualified to make that judgment.

You need to see a doctor whenever you experience bleeding—physically or spiritually. The Bible explains this in Romans 8:26-27:

Likewise the Spirit also helpeth our infirmities: for we know not what we should pray for as we ought: but the Spirit itself maketh intercession for us with groaning which cannot be uttered. And he that searcheth the heart knoweth what is the mind of the Spirit, because he maketh intercession for the saints according to the will of God

God knows you better than you know yourself; that's why you need to keep a close relationship with Him. Not only does He love you, but He is the one who impregnated you, so He knows everything that is going on inside you. He's not like that no-good man who walked out on you when he found out you were pregnant, or that woman who thought that because she was the one carrying the child, she didn't have to tell you about it until she was ready. God is a loving father who cares about you and the baby.

Hold on—you just finished your first trimester. This is an exciting time for you, even with all the changes you are going through. I know you can't wait to have this baby, but there are still two more trimesters to go. The best is yet to come.

CHAPTER SEVEN

SECOND TRIMESTER

At each stage of pregnancy, the growing baby is not the same as he or she was just a few weeks earlier. Each stage brings new considerations and concerns. While the first trimester is critical for the development of the organs, with greater concern over the possibility of miscarriage, and the third trimester centers on the baby's maturation and the delivery process, the second trimester is a reprieve of sorts, a time many women find enjoyable.

Weeks thirteen through twenty-four of pregnancy are a time when a woman has the peace of mind to educate herself about having a baby. By now she has become somewhat accustomed to the strain on her body, physical symptoms like morning sickness have usually eased, and prenatal visits are usually just routine checks to ensure that the pregnancy is progressing as expected.

Of course, the obstetrician is actually doing a lot more than the mother realizes during these "well-pregnancy" visits. The fetal heart rate is assessed, and the baby's size is estimated and compared to the size recorded during previous visits, to make sure the baby has grown appropriately.

Congratulations! The fact that you've made it this far means you've done all the right things. You have not aborted or miscarried, and all the changes to your body didn't kill you. Remember, *whatever doesn't kill you only makes you stronger.*

There are three parts to this stage of pregnancy, and all three are extremely important: changes, rest, and possible complications. Let's look at these three areas.

The baby should be growing rapidly at this point, so the mother should make sure she schedules regular visits to her doctor, who will check to make sure that the baby is growing at a normal pace. As in the first trimester, the baby needs to be growing constantly to be healthy.

The mother will notice changes not only to her baby, but to herself as well. The second trimester is when her body really begins to expand. Stretch marks begin, although they might be invisible at first. And everything that was already there grows! Moles get bigger, skin tags get bigger, and even warts can get bigger. Thanks to estrogen, everything has a better blood supply.

The same thing will happen with your spiritual pregnancy. Just as a woman's body changes and she begins to see all the moles, stretch marks, and warts, you will begin to notice all the things about you that displease the Lord. Everything you do now will seem magnified.

Let's see what Paul tells the Corinthian church:

> **Now the Lord is that Spirit: and where the Spirit of the Lord is, there is liberty. But we all, with open face beholding as in a glass the glory of the Lord, are changed into the same image from glory to glory, even as by the Spirit of the Lord.**
>
> **2 Cor. 3:17-18 (King James Bible)**

Paul is explaining here that whenever you come to Christ, there should be a change, because the Lord makes you free. The law kills, but the Spirit gives life.

This is why you are experiencing so many changes—because that same Spirit impregnated you, and where the Spirit is, there is liberty.

Just as a baby grows inside the mother, your God-given purpose is growing inside of you. And for every inch that the baby grows, there must be changes. Remember, *tradition is an enemy to revelation.* The longer you are pregnant, the more the Lord will change you.

At this point, you should be noticing the changes. You don't go to the places you used to go; you don't talk the way you used to talk. I remember my grandmother putting it this way: "I looked at my hands and they looked new. I looked at my feet and they did, too." Of course, those things didn't actually happen. That was the only way Grandmother could explain the changes she was experiencing.

Are you going through the same thing? Don't worry—you're right on track. Remember what Paul says in 2 Corinthians 5:17:

Therefore if any man be in Christ, he is a new creature: old things are passed away; behold, all things are become new.

Paul is not saying that the moment you are saved, everything about you will automatically change. He is saying that there should be a process already taking place—sanctification, the process of being set apart. You have been set apart to have that child, to serve God's purpose, and it will involve a process of change.

I like to call this trimester between one and three "the in-between." This is when you actually can get a little rest.

The second trimester gives a pregnant woman a break. The first and the third trimester are usually times of intense worry. If the big, bad concerns are ruled out, the second trimester affords the pregnant woman the opportunity to rejoin the world after the initial frights of the first twelve weeks.

This is the time to enjoy the fact that you are pregnant. Now is when you can begin decorating the baby's room and plan all the things you will need when the new baby arrives. This is also the time when you can get some needed rest.

Notice that after the disciples did all that Jesus asked of them, He told them to rest:

And the apostles gathered themselves together unto Jesus, and told him all things, both what they had done, and what they had taught. And he said unto them, come ye yourself apart into a desert place, and rest awhile: for there were many coming and going, and they had no leisure so much as to eat.

Mark 6:30-31(King James Bible)

Jesus sent the disciples out to preach the gospel, and upon their return they began to tell Him about all the things they experienced. The one thing I want you to notice here is that He instructs them to get some rest. Just as it was very important that they rested their bodies, it is also important that you get the rest your body needs.

This is the point in your pregnancy when you can relax awhile. I'm not suggesting that you become lazy, but everyone needs proper rest in order to function properly in this world. You need to take some time to enjoy where you are right now and spend some quality time with the Lord.

God made us the way He did on purpose; our bodies require rest. Even Jesus took some time to relax and enjoy the company of His friends and family, so don't let anyone tell you that something is wrong with "down time." There is a long road ahead, so you'd better get it while you can. I don't have to tell you that when the baby comes, there will be hardly any time to take a break. This is the time to kick back and let your hair down, to take a trip or just go for a ride. You can't carry the burdens of this pregnancy around with you all the time; you need to let go and have a little fun. (You do remember what that is, don't you?)

Notice what God did when He finished creating the world:

Thus the heavens and the earth were finished, and all the host of them. And on the seventh day God ended his work which he had made; and he rested on the seventh day from all his work which he had made. And God blessed the seventh day, and sanctified it: because that in it he had rested from all his work which God created and made.

Gen. 2:1-3 (King James Bible)

Even when God made the world, He rested. Now, God did not need any rest—He was setting an example for us. To say that God *needed* rest would put Him in the same category as you or me, and He is not a human being. I don't want to serve a God that's human—do you? Thank goodness He's not a man, but the only living and true God.

When God rested, He was commanding everyone to rest and worship Him. He didn't want any work done on that day of rest; all He wanted man to do was to worship Him. And still today, He expects you to give Him a day of worship, whether it's Saturday or Sunday. You need to set time apart to worship Him.

Let's see what Jesus says about rest in Matthew 11:28-30:

Come unto me, all ye that labor and are heavy laden, and I will give you rest. Take my yoke upon you, and learn of me: for I am meek and lowly in heart: and ye shall find rest unto your souls. For my yoke is easy, and my burden is light.

In biblical times, a farmer plowing his field would place a yoke around the necks of his mules to get them to go where he wanted them to. It was a heavy yoke they had to bear, but Jesus says here that if you take His yoke, you will find that it's not hard. He is a loving master who wants only the best for His servants; He won't whip you into submission. In fact, the only true rest you can have is in Him. He is the only one who offers rest to the body, soul, and spirit.

I remember my grandfather taking his mules out into the field and working them hard to make the crops. It would be early in the morning when he started; only the animals were up, and he worked them.

Jesus is saying here that the only thing that should be working like a dog is a dog. He never intended for people to be treated like animals.

What I love about Jesus is that He always explained things in terms that the people could understand. I'm sure there were farmers among those listening to Him, and He knew they would understand his message when He put it this way. In short, He was talking about becoming one of his disciples.

PREMATURE DELIVERY

With some pregnancies, there is a threat that the child could be born prematurely. This can happen when the cervix just doesn't have the strength to stay closed any longer, dilating painlessly (without contractions) and leading to a premature delivery. To safeguard against this possibility, the doctor might advise the patient to be on prolonged bed rest.

In a case like that, there's nothing the mother can do except follow the doctor's orders and get some rest. This is a frightening time for her—she's facing the possibility of losing the child she has been carrying. If a baby is delivered in the second trimester, its chances of survival are slim.

This situation can also happen in the spiritual sense, when you feel that you don't have the strength to go any further—the baby is about to come, and there is nothing you can do about it. Perhaps the devil has brought all kinds of attacks upon your life, and you are almost out of strength. If you follow the doctor's orders, however, everything will be all right.

We are assured of God's healing grace in 1 Peter 5:10:

But the God of all grace, who hath called us into his eternal glory by Christ Jesus, after that ye have suffered a while, make you perfect, establish, strengthen, settle you.

God will give you the strength you need to make it; He's there for you. There's nothing that you will go through that He doesn't already know. He will not allow the baby to come before it is time. *He holds the due date in His hand.*

Finally, my brethren, be strong in the Lord, and in the power of his might.

Eph. 6:10 (King James Bible)

This battle is a spiritual one, so you must draw your strength from the Lord.

THE PLACENTA (AFTERBIRTH)

Let's look at the placenta and its importance. The placenta, or afterbirth, usually settles into a permanent spot during the second trimester, while the rest of the uterus expands away from the site of its implantation. But if that site is over the baby's exit route, this not only prevents natural delivery but also creates a potentially fatal problem. The placenta is a highly vascular organ. If it tears away as the cervix thins, it will cause hemorrhaging that endangers both mother and child.

In a normal pregnancy, the placenta wraps around the child and allows it to take nourishment from the mother. But this organ that is designed to protect and nourish can also complicate delivery and even endanger the life of the mother and child.

At this stage of pregnancy, you need to be very careful. Get plenty of rest, but stay informed about your pregnancy.

THE POSITION OF THE PLACENTA

Remember, where the placenta is positioned can determine the outcome of the pregnancy. If it's in the wrong place, it can endanger the life of the mother and baby. If it's in the right place, it will protect and nourish the baby right up to delivery.

Think about that fact as we look at the story of the devil:

How art thou fallen from heaven, o Lucifer, son of the morning! How art thou cut down to the ground, which didst weaken the nations! For thou hast said in thou heart, I will ascend into heaven,

I will exalt my throne above the stars of God: I will sit also upon the mount of the congregation, in the sides of the north: I will ascend above the heights of the clouds; I will be like the most high. Yet thou shalt be brought down to hell, to the sides of the pits.

Isa. 14:12-15 (King James Bible)

Notice how the devil is giving himself all the praise and wanting what doesn't belong to him. He wants to be God, but He was created to give and bring glory to God. The Bible says Lucifer was beautiful, with pipes coming from him. Clearly, he was set apart to worship God, but he got caught up in desiring praise instead of giving it. In this passage, Satan uses the words *I* or *my* six times; everything that comes out of his mouth is directed back toward him. His placenta was in the wrong place, and it hurt not only him but also one third of the angels in heaven. This world is hemorrhaging because of him.

You were created to give God praise and glory. He also impregnated you with purpose. Don't let that purpose hurt you. Remember that the very gift that He gave you to bless someone else can turn around and hurt you and others. So don't get caught up in all the compliments when people tell you how well you do whatever it is God asks you to do. Give the glory to God.

When people take credit for the gift God gave them, I call this *misplaced placenta*. If you want to get to the next stage of pregnancy, don't misplace your placenta. *An afterbirth blessing can turn into a pre-birth curse.*

There is a life inside you whose health depends on the position of the placenta. Don't be like the devil; let your position, glorifying God, be made known. Your baby is depending on it.

Listen to God's warning to Israel:

Shall I bring to the birth, and not cause to bring forth? Saith the Lord: shall I cause to bring forth, and shut the womb? Saith thy God.

Isa. 66:9 (King James Bible)

Remember, where your placenta is positioned—where your praise is focused—will determine how your baby develops in this stage. Don't allow anything or anyone to block your praise. This is what the devil will try to do—he will send people into your life to prevent you from glorifying God. You have to be determined not to let that happen. There is an old saying that goes, "If you don't want to go, get out of my way—don't hinder me." Let the devil know there's something inside you that has to get out. Don't stop now. Keep on moving.

Although this is a time of rest, don't get too relaxed and lose focus on what's important: your baby.

The spot you pick now will determine the path you take tomorrow.

CHAPTER EIGHT
THIRD TRIMESTER

Hang in there—you've almost made it. You have already made it through two trimesters, and this will be the last, although you should continue to be very careful. During prenatal visits in the last trimester, the doctor monitors the health of mother and baby through fetal surveillance and fetal activity determination.

FETAL SURVEILLANCE

Thanks to ultrasound, doctors can now see babies before they are born; guesses about the baby's growth have been replaced by exact measurements. And while doctors still generally use a physical exam to determine the baby's position, an ultrasound can confirm that judgment.

Ultrasounds are used to measure amniotic fluid, one of the most crucial indicators of fetal well-being, and to directly observe fetal movements, which reassure the mother-to-be of her baby's good health.

During these final prenatal visits, the doctor checks the baby's position as well as its vital signs, which are just as important, as a lack of vital signs can indicate that the baby has died and will be stillborn—a devastating experience for parents.

It is important that you make sure that your vision stays alive, so check it regularly for vital signs. If anyone is excited about your future, it should be you. If it seems to be taking too long for the vision to come to pass, just remember what God says in Hab. 2:2-3:

And the lord answered me, and said, write the vision, and make it plain upon tables, that he may

run that readeth it. For the vision is yet for an appointed time, but at the end it shall speak, and not lie: though it tarry, wait for it; because it will surely come, it will not tarry.

Just as an ultrasound will show the size and position of a baby at this stage, your vision should do the same thing for you. That's why the Lord asks you to write it down—so you can look at it whenever you need encouragement.

Fetal surveillance technology is designed to monitor a baby's growth and movements. Your spiritual vision is designed to monitor your spiritual growth and movements. At this stage of pregnancy—physical or spiritual—the baby should be moving along fine.

Listen to what the Bible says about growth:

Of whom we have many things to say, and hard to be uttered, seeing ye are dull of hearing. For when for the times ye ought to be teachers, ye have need that one teach you again which be the first principles of the oracles of God; and are become such as have need of milk, and not of strong meat. For everyone that useth milk is unskillful in the word of righteousness: for he is a baby. But strong meat belongeth to them that are of full age, even those by reason of use have their senses exercised to discern both good and evil.

Heb. 5:11-14 (King James Bible)

Paul is telling the Hebrews that they have failed to mature as Christians—that when they should have been teaching others about God, they instead needed someone to teach them. He calls them babies, saying they can't eat "strong meat" because of their lack of knowledge.

By this time you should be mature as a Christian—certainly more mature than you were last trimester. This is a crucial point, because you will never deliver that child if you are not ready. So you need to stop and survey your growth in the Lord. Remember, this is the last stage of your spiritual pregnancy; your baby is about to make its entrance into the world. Are you ready?

FETAL ACTIVITY DETERMINATION

The fetal activity determination (FAD) is a valuable measurement of fetal movement in relation to fetal heart rate.

When you run around the block, your heart races as your body speeds oxygenated blood to the areas that need it, your muscles. (It's a good thing our organs work together like this, or many of us would drop dead just chasing after the dog that got out again!) In the same way, when a baby moves in utero (as indicated on the fetal monitor), there should be a rise in the fetal heart rate. In other words, the baby's vital signs should correspond to its movements.

Similarly, during your FAD—Faith, Anointing, Destiny—everything should be working together. All your actions should line up with your Faith, Anointing, and Destiny. Let's look at each of them and see where you stand.

FAITH

> **What doth it profit, my brethren, though a man say he has faith, and have not works? Can faith save him? If a brother or sister be naked, and destitute without food, And one of you say unto them, depart in peace, be ye warm and filled; notwithstanding ye give them not those things which are needful to the body; what doth it profit? Even so faith, if it has not works, is dead, being alone. Yea, a man may say, thou hast faith, and I have works: show me thou faith without thou works, and I will show thee my faith by my works. Thou believest that there is a God; thou doest well: the devil also believe, and tremble. But will thou know, o vain man, that faith without works is dead?**

> **James 2:14-20 (King James Bible)**

James is emphasizing the importance of having *working* faith. It's not enough just to have faith, he says; your faith must be put into action.

Faith is the thing that will get you where you need to be. Without it, you won't have the drive to get there. For inspiration, read Hebrews 11, which lists the things that some of the patriots did in the past with their faith. Your faith walk should be leading you down the path to your new future. You should be doing everything you can to prepare for the arrival of your baby.

One of the mistakes expectant parents make is failing to prepare adequately for their baby. They know their baby will arrive soon, but still there's no food, clothing, room, diapers, bottles, or money.

Your faith should show through what you do, not what you say. If the baby in you is alive, then your faith should be alive, too. Your faith should be feeding your work, and your work should be feeding your faith.

Listen to what the Bible says about faith:

But without faith it is impossible to please him: for he that cometh to God must believe that he is, and that he is a rewarder of them that diligently seek him.

Heb. 11:6 (King James Bible)

You cannot please God without having faith in Him. How's your faith? Are you leaning on Him for everything? Do you believe that He will take you through this pregnancy? If you answered yes to these questions, you're on your way.

ANOINTING

To *anoint* means to authorize someone or set someone apart for a particular work or service. In biblical references, the anointed person belongs to God in a special sense. Anointing in the New Testament refers to anointing through the Holy Spirit, which brings understanding. This anointing is not only for kings, priest, and prophets; it is for everyone who believes in the Lord Jesus Christ. The anointing occurs physically, with a substance like oil, myrrh, or balsam. But there is also a spiritual dimension, as the Holy Spirit anoints a person's heart and mind with the love and truth of God.

Listen to what Jesus says about anointing in Luke 4:18:

The Spirit of the Lord is upon me, because he has anointed me to preach the gospel to the poor; he hath sent me to heal the broken hearted, to preach deliverance to the captive, and recovering of sight to the blind, to set at liberty them that are bruised.

At this point in scripture, Jesus is starting His ministry and goes into the temple to proclaim that He has been anointed to preach the gospel, heal the broken-hearted, preach deliverance to the captive, give sight to the blind, and free those who are bruised. Notice that Jesus says He was *anointed* to do these things—He knows exactly what His purpose is and He has been anointed to do it. God anoints you to do His will. You have been anointed to carry your baby. The act of anointing ensures that you accomplish God's will for your life.

In the Old Testament, the Spirit comes upon God's people as they perform certain duties for Him; He comes upon them, and then He leaves. In the New Testament, the Spirit lives on the inside the believer. Everyone who is born again has the Spirit inside him or her. It is your job to allow the Spirit to control you and to accept the gifts that He has for you.

It is important in this stage that you have been anointed to perform your responsibility. You cannot do what you're not anointed to do, because the Spirit gives you the ability to do what you normally couldn't. This is when God puts His *super* on your *natural* and gives you supernatural ability.

Let's read what John says about the Holy Spirit in 1 John 2:20:

> **But ye have an unction from the Holy one, and ye know all things.**

John goes on to say that the Spirit, once received, lives inside you:

> **But the anointing which ye have received of him abideth in you, and ye need not that any man teach you: but as the same anointing teacheth you of all things, and is truth, and is no lie, and even as it hath taught you, ye shall abide in him.**
>
> **1 John 2:27 (King James Bible)**

At this stage in your spiritual pregnancy, the Holy Spirit will anoint you like never before. He will begin to teach you the things of the Lord, and you will remember everything you've studied and learned. Your faith and your anointing need to be working together at a high level—that is, you should have faith that God will give you the ability (anointing) to do what He's asked of you.

DESTINY

You were destined to have this baby. It's your calling, your life purpose, the reason you were born, and there is no stopping you now. You're in the last stage of your destiny. Your faith is greater than it's ever been, and you know you're anointed for the task. Everything leading up to this point was intended to prepare you for this. If you experienced a crisis along the way, don't curse it. *Crisis is a springboard to your destiny.* All the things you have experienced up to this point were just a set-up.

Remember, God has a way of working out every situation for your good. Let's see what Paul tells the church in Rome:

And we know that all things work together for good to them that love God, to them who are called according to his purpose. For whom he did foreknow, he also did predestine to conform to the image of his son, that he might be the first born among many brethren. Moreover whom he did predestine, them he also called: and whom he called, them he also justified: and whom he justified, them he also glorified.

Rom. 8:28-30 (King James Bible)

Here Paul explains that everything you experience is part of God's plan for your life. Everything that has happened, every situation is divinely planned for your good.

In Romans 8:26, Paul says that the Spirit helps our infirmities and helps us in our ignorance. This is Faith, Anointing, and Destiny working together to help you get to the next level. This is your FAD test.

In this final stage of pregnancy, everything needs to be working together well. You should be at a high spiritual level, ready to deliver that baby.

LAMAZE COACH

By now, you should have someone who can work with you during this final stage, someone who is going down the same road and trying to reach the same destination, someone who understands what you're carrying. You don't want someone who's envious of you and your baby. It is important to have somebody you can talk to, someone who can share in the experience with you.

Most pregnant women have their husband or a friend or family member serve as their Lamaze coach. The coach is there to help the woman with breathing during delivery; he or she is a strong mental help, as well.

According to Romans 15:1, we should help and support one another:

> **We then that are strong ought to bear the infirmities of the weak, and not to please ourselves.**

When you are feeling weak, you need someone who can be strong without throwing it in your face—someone who doesn't support you out of self-interest, but only wants to help you. Let's see what James says:

> **Confess your faults one to another, and pray one for another, that ye may be healed. The effectual**

fervent prayer of a righteous man availeth much.

James 5:16 (King James Bible)

Simply put, you need a prayer partner, someone who will have your best interest at heart and won't gossip about you. The final stage of your pregnancy will be a lot easier if you have a prayer partner by your side. Pray and ask the Lord to lead you to someone.

MY LAMAZE COACHES

I thank God that throughout my entire life, He has surrounded me with people who have had my best interest at heart. I thank Him every day for the lasting impression these individuals made in my life. I would like to tell you about all the people who have impacted my life. They have been my Lamaze coaches.

First and foremost are my parents, Ennis and Yvonne Antoine. I thank God that He gave me two parents who provided and cared for me. They have always been an inspiration in my life. If it had not been for my parents, I wouldn't have had all the advantages in life that I enjoyed. They loved and nourished me, leading me to Christ and serving as irreplaceable examples for me. My father was also my pastor; he was called to start a church in the West Bank area of New Orleans. He served faithfully there for fifteen years until his death; my mother served faithfully by his side until her death. Together they accomplished great things for the Kingdom and laid a firm foundation for me to continue their work.

The late Reverend Joseph Howard Sr. of New Zion Baptist Church was my first pastor. My parents became a part of his church, and after that, my life would never be the same. Pastor Howard always told me that God had something special for me to do. I didn't agree or understand at the time, but I now know that he was my second Lamaze coach. He put the thought into my head that there was something more I should be seeking from God. He strongly believed that God gave each of us gifts to be used for His purpose.

Reverend Austin Dennis was my third Lamaze coach. He became the pastor of New Zion Baptist Church after Pastor Howard passed away. I learned endurance, perseverance, patience, and faithfulness from Pastor Dennis. When we were looking for a pastor to replace Pastor Howard, I watched him come to the church and go through the process with dignity and grace. I must also include the church family at New Zion for being so loving and caring as my family became a part of theirs.

Bishop Darryl S. Brister was my fourth Lamaze coach. After becoming a pastor myself, I began to search for a young man whom God was using in a different way, so that I could learn more about Him. The Lord led me to Bishop Brister. He taught me how to minister with an excellent spirit. He mentored me, allowing me to glean knowledge from him. I have never experienced excellence like this before. His congregation had eight thousand members and several locations. I began to dream about the greater possibilities for my life.

I thank God for my spiritual parents, Bishop I. V. Hilliard and Pastor Bridget Hilliard. They have been an inspiration in my life as I've watched how they work together and love each other. I have learned so much from them about ministry; what I've learned has helped me become a better pastor, father, and husband. I compare my relationship with them to that of Elizabeth and Mary—every time I'm in their presence, my baby leaps inside me! At the time of this writing, they are serving as my final Lamaze coach. I have been ministering under their leadership for the last six years, and the experience has changed my life tremendously. I continue to learn church and leadership principles from them that have taken my church to new levels.

As you can see, I have been blessed to have some wonderful people in my life who have helped me develop into the person I am today.

FINAL CHANGE

It is in this last stage of pregnancy that final changes must be made—any problems that could affect the baby must be addressed.

Preeclampsia—a dangerous condition characterized by a spike in blood pressure—is typically a third trimester problem, but it can develop earlier. If it does, that's a sign that the preeclampsia will become fairly severe.

Other conditions that may develop later in pregnancy may cause less concern but are still noticeable and bothersome. For example, the menstrual-like cramps some women experience during the first trimester are often replaced by pain in the "round ligaments," which originate on the sides of the uterus, run through the inguinal canals, and insert on the side of the vaginal walls and even the inner thighs. As these ligaments are pretty loosely supported even when the uterus is the size of a pear, they can become a nuisance when the uterus gets considerably larger in the second and third trimesters. The uterus can actually shift from side to side, aggravating the round ligaments and causing pain on one or both sides where the hips join the abdomen. It is a harmless condition, but the pain can be alarming, stopping a pregnant woman dead in her tracks. Usually she can lessen the discomfort temporarily by changing positions, but the only final cure is childbirth.

Is there anything that is giving you a lot of pain? Do you find it hard to relax? Are you experiencing pain from every side? There may be some final changes that need to take place. We can find a good example of this scenario in the story of Jacob:

And Jacob was left alone; and there wrestled a man with him until the breaking of the day. And when he saw that he prevailed not against him, he touched the hollow of his thigh; and the hollow of Jacob's thigh was out of joint, as he wrestled with him. And he said, let me go, for the day breaketh. And he said, I will not let thee go, except thou bless me. And he said unto him, what is thou name? And he said, Jacob. And he said, thou name shall

be called no more Jacob, but Israel: for as a prince hast thou power with God and with men, and has prevailed. And Jacob asked him, and said, tell me, I pray thee, thy name. And he said, wherefore is it that thou doest ask after my name? And he blessed him there. And Jacob called the name of the place Peniel: for I have seen God face to face, and my life is preserved. And as he passed over Penuel the sun rose upon him, and he halted upon his thigh.

Gen. 32:24–31(King James Bible)

In the final stages in Jacob's life, God had to deal with Jacob before He blessed him. Jacob had to make some changes in his life. You see in the story that Jacob wrestles with the angel all night long, demanding that the angel bless him. Jacob is so determined to get that blessing that he refuses to let go until the angel complies. When the angel sees that he can't prevail against Jacob, he touches the hollow of Jacob's thigh. This is a significant detail. I submit to you that there was a reason the angel touched Jacob's thigh.

When someone made an oath in Old Testament days, it was customary for him to put his hand under the thigh of the one who required him to swear by his word. We can find examples of this custom in the book of Genesis (The Amplified Bible):

And Abraham said to the eldest servant of his house [*Eliezer of Damascus*], who ruled over all that he had, I beg of you, put your hand under my thigh . . .

Gen. 24:2 (The Amplified Bible)

So the servant put his hand under the thigh of Abraham
his master and swore to him concerning this matter.

Gen 24:9 (**The Amplified Bible)**

When the time drew near that Israel must die, he called
his son Joseph and said to him, If now I have found favor
in your sight, put your hand under my thigh and [*promise
to*] deal loyally and faithfully with me. Do not bury me,
I beg of you, in Egypt,

Gen. 47:29 (**The Amplified Bible)**

You see, the thigh is connected to the organs of
procreation, so this custom was a visual reminder that if the
person didn't follow through with his oath, the other party
would seek justice, or his offspring would. So by touching
Jacob's thigh, the angel is breaking generational curses.
All through Jacob's bloodline were liars. His grandfather
and father were liars, and even the name *Jacob* means
"supplanter" and "trickster." Jacob had spent his whole life
getting over on people. God had to change that.

Notice that the next thing that the angel does here is ask
Jacob to say his name. Now, the angel already knows his name;
he just wants Jacob to say it, because it means something—it
means he is a liar and a trickster. And confession is good for
the soul. After Jacob says his name, the angel changes it to
Israel, meaning "a prince with God."

It's so important to God that your baby's lineage is
straight that He will change you to ensure the integrity of
your baby. That's why you're going through the various

experiences of spiritual pregnancy—you need to make all the necessary changes before delivering your baby.

According to the Bible, Jacob limped on that leg after his night of wrestling with the angel. I believe the limp was meant to show physically what happened to Jacob spiritually. In the same way, you'll find that some of your life experiences will leave you with scars you will not be able to hide; you will carry them around your whole life. Don't worry about those scars. They are just a testimony of where you came from and evidence of where you're going. And they might just help someone else along the way.

Just as a pregnant woman has to change her position to get relief from pain, you will have to change spiritually to get relief before your baby gets here.

CHAPTER NINE

DELIVERY

Delivery is the process by which the baby is expelled from the uterus, through the birth canal, and into the world. It begins with uterine contractions that occur irregularly, every twenty to thirty minutes; as labor progresses, the contractions increase in frequency and severity. The usual length of labor is thirteen to fourteen hours for a first-time mother, and eight to nine hours for a woman who has given birth previously. The duration of labor can vary widely, however.

This is it! You have made it to the final step of your spiritual pregnancy, and your baby is about to make its entrance into the world. I know that you can hardly wait. It's been a long time coming, and there is a lot of anticipation. So hold on—there are just a few more difficulties you will have to endure, and then it will all be over. If this is your first time, prepare yourself for a long delivery.

WATER BREAK

When a pregnant woman's water breaks, it's a sign that her baby is ready to be delivered. When the amniotic sac breaks, the baby is ready for its entrance into the world. The placenta that's been providing protection and nourishment is becoming depleted, and the baby has outgrown its present space. This is when the mother heads for the hospital.

A baby can't live in utero forever; it needs to come into the world. That's why God allows a baby to stay inside its mother for only nine months. Then it's time for the world to enjoy the blessing she's been carrying around.

Has your water broken?

Do you find yourself crying all the time, or weeping in spirit because of the things going on around you? Is your heart broken over situations that seem helpless? There is a reason for this: your water is breaking, and it's time for your baby to come into the world. The very thing that is breaking your heart is the problem your baby was designed to solve. Your water will break to get it here.

You are never passionate about things that don't matter to you. The only things that move you are the ones you care about. That's why you had to go through all that hell—to make you passionate about your purpose, so when your water broke, you would be ready. Remember, even Jesus cried:

Jesus wept.

John 11:35 (King James Bible)

This is the shortest verse in the Bible. It took only two words to explain what Jesus was feeling. He was not crying because Lazarus was dead, but because the people didn't have faith in the power of God. It was God's plan for Jesus to be there when He was. He could have made it to Lazarus in time to save him, but it was God's plan for Jesus to come after Lazarus died. According to the Bible, Jesus waited four days to go, because people believed that after three days, the soul left the body. In fact, the Bible says that the body had begun to stink. Jesus wanted to make sure that the people knew that Lazarus was dead and that He had the power to resurrect him.

Because Jesus's water broke, a miracle took place: He raised Lazarus from the grave.

Water breaking on the outside is an indication of what's happening on the inside. Water can never break unless there life inside.

Let's see what Jesus says about Himself as "the life":

Jesus said unto her, I am the resurrection, and the life: he that believeth in me, though he were dead, yet shall he live.

John 11:25 (King James Bible)

Jesus delivered a miracle right there, amidst the people. His water broke, and the miracle came out. Water brings life.

Turn again, and tell Hezekiah the captain of my people, thus saith the Lord, the God of David thy father, I have heard thy prayer, I have seen thy tears: behold, I will heal thee: on the third day thou shalt go up unto the house of the Lord.

2 Kings 20:5 (King James Bible)

In this passage, Hezekiah is very sick and has been told by the prophet Isaiah that he is going to die. When Isaiah leaves, Hezekiah begins to pray and cry—and because his water breaks, God gives him fifteen more years. I'm not saying that all you have to do is cry to get God's blessing. Remember, it's what on the inside that gives life on the outside. You can cry until the cows come home, but it won't do you a bit of good if your heart is messed up.

I submit to you that Hezekiah already had another fifteen years of life inside him; he just needed his water to break to bring forth that life. I'm talking about real repentance! Consider these passages from the book of Psalms:

Thou tellest my wanderings: put thou my tears into thy bottle: are they not in thy book?

Psalms 56:8 (King James Bible)

They that sow in tears shall reap in joy. He that goeth forth and weepeth, bearing precious seed, shall doubtless come again with rejoicing, bringing his sheaves with him.

Psalms 126:5 (King James Bible)

God loves you so much that every time you cry, He puts your tears in a bottle. Every time your water breaks, He remembers it.

LIFE IN THE WATER

There is life in water. Each water molecule consists of two parts hydrogen and one part oxygen. Notice that water is made up of three parts, just as God is Father, Son and Holy Spirit. And water has three forms, solid, liquid, and vapor, just as you have three forms, body, soul, and spirit.

Water represents the life that the Spirit brings. The Spirit is the water, and when you have one person in the trinity, you have all three, the Father, the Son, and the Holy Spirit.

Jesus answered and said unto her, if thou knewest the gift of God, and who it is that saith unto thee, give me to drink; thou wouldest have asked of him, and he would have given thee living water. But whosoever drinketh of the water that I shall give him shall never thirst; but the water that I shall give him be in him a well of water springing up into everlasting life.

John 4:10-14 (King James Bible)

Jesus is trying to get the Samaritan woman to see that He offers living water—water that will never run out, that will live inside her like a well.

Just as water can take three forms, Jesus takes three forms in scripture. In Daniel 3:25, He becomes a solid, cooling the flames. In John 19:34, water and blood pour from Him. In John 20:19, He becomes like vapor and walks through the walls.

There is a song I love with a lyrical reference to water: "As the deer panteth for the water, oh my soul longest after thee." Water protects the deer three ways—it offers a place to hide, it covers the deer's scent, and it hides the deer's tracks. Just as the deer runs to the water, you should run to the Lord when the devil is in hot pursuit of you.

Now that your water has broken, get ready for life to come forward. Don't panic, just let the Spirit take you to the next step, and everything will be all right.

CONTRACTIONS

During labor, contractions take place every twenty to thirty minutes, increasing in frequency and severity as the baby gets closer to delivery. Before that, however, a pregnant woman generally experiences pre-labor, a period of irregular uterine contractions during which the cervix thins, softens, and may begin to dilate.

The birth process has three stages. Let's take a look at all three and see where you are and what you will have to go through.

STAGE ONE

As the body prepares for delivery, the uterus contracts strongly and regularly, the cervix dilates with each contraction, and the baby's head rotates to fit through the mother's pelvis.

Notice that three things happen in the first stage: stronger, more regular contractions, dilation of the cervix, and rotation of the baby's head.

At this stage you will feel a strong need to get your baby here, and those feelings will occur on a regular basis. They will always be on your mind. You will become consumed with the thought of delivering your baby.

Do you find yourself always thinking about what the Lord has put inside you? Do you feel such a strong need to do His will for your life that you are not satisfied doing anything else?

With every contraction there is a need to push. This is the Lord causing you to dilate, getting you ready for the delivery. In order for your child to come, you will have to make room for it to get here, because everything in your life is enlarging. Not only do you dilate, but the head must rotate to begin its exit. God's purpose for you has now become the focus, the head of your life.

And they came to a place, which was named Gethsemane: and he said to his disciples, sit ye here, while I shall pray. And he takes with him Peter and James and John, and began to be sore amazed, and to be very heavy; And said unto them, my soul is exceedingly sorrowful unto death: tarry ye here, and watch. And he went forward a little, and fell on the ground, and prayed that, if it were possible, the hour may pass from him. And he said, abba, father, all things are possible unto thee; take away this cup from me, nevertheless not what I will, but what thou will.

Mark 14:32-36 (King James Bible)

Jesus is talking to his father in the garden of Gethsemane. The word *gethsemane* means "winepress"—a place where winemakers would press the grapes. God brought Jesus to Gethsemane to press their wills together. Notice that Jesus is in so much labor pain that He is "exceedingly sorrowful unto death." He is carrying the salvation of the world inside Him, and when His contractions begin, He feels it.

Mothers, you can be a witness to what contractions feel like; the pain is so unbearable that you feel like dying. This is what Jesus felt, ten times over. He had more than one baby in Him; in fact, He carried everyone who would ever live. I submit to you that Jesus actually died in the garden of Gethsemane. Now, I know that his physical death took place on the cross, but His will died in the garden, when His will merged with God's. Paul touches on this in Galatians:

> **I have been crucified with Christ [*in Him I have shared His crucifixion*]; it is no longer I who live, but Christ (the Messiah) lives in me; and the life I now live in the body I live by faith in (by adherence to and reliance on and complete trust in) the Son of God, Who loved me and gave Himself up for me.**
>
> **Gal. 2:20 (The Amplified Bible)**

STAGE TWO

As labor intensifies, the mother bears down in response to pressure against her pelvic muscles, and the crown of the baby's head becomes visible in the widened birth canal. As the head emerges entirely, the physician turns the baby's shoulders, which emerge one at a time with the next contraction. The rest of the body then slides out relatively easily, and the umbilical cord is sealed and cut.

During this final stage of delivery, it will seem that everything around you has begun to go crazy. This is when you will need to bear down and push, because the devil will not just sit back and let you have your baby. He will begin to fight you like never before.

Remember, no matter how hard it gets, don't stop pushing. You will have to push your way through, even though you will be experiencing pain like never before.

I press toward the mark for the prize of the high calling of God in Christ Jesus.

Phil. 3:14 (King James Bible)

In this scripture, Paul wants so badly to receive his baby that he says, in effect, "I don't care how hard it gets—I'm pushing." Paul vows to forget everything that's behind him and press forward. And because of his determination to move forward—because he pushed every time he felt contractions—we now enjoy thirteen books credited to Paul.

A pregnant woman pushes in response to pressure. You must do the same. Every time you feel the pressure, push. Every time someone talks about you, push. Every time someone hurts you, push.

It is at this point that the baby's head becomes visible. You will begin to actually see the first part of your vision. It will materialize right before your eyes.

STAGE THREE

The third stage occurs within ten minutes of the baby's birth. The uterus continues to contract, expelling the severed umbilical cord and placenta.

The contractions won't stop until everything is out; you will have to release everything in order for them to stop.

CUTTING THE UMBILICAL CORD

The umbilical cord allows a fetus to be nourished as it grows and develops within the womb. In the same way, God allowed you to feed your baby as long as it was inside you, but now that it's out, you will have to cut the cord. Metaphorically speaking, this is one of the hardest things for mothers to do; they feel it's their job always to be connected to their child, providing support. But God wants you to cut the cord because He doesn't want anything that He gives you to come between you and Him. Sometimes when God blesses you, you hold onto the blessing harder than you do Him. There is a danger of turning that child, that blessing, into a god. Remember, whatever He gave you to do won't crash and die if you're not around.

> **And they came to the place which God had told him of; and Abraham built an altar there, and laid the wood in order, and bound Isaac his son, and laid him on the altar upon the wood. And Abraham stretched forth his hand, and took the knife to slay his son. And the angel of the Lord called unto him out of the heavens, and said, Abraham, Abraham: and he said, here am I. And he said, lay not thine hand upon the lad, neither do thou anything unto him: for now I know that thou fearest God, seeing thou has not withheld thy son, thine only son from me.**
>
> **Gen. 22:9-12 (King James Bible)**

God is testing Abraham to see if he loves Isaac more than Him. God wants to know whether Abraham will put the child in front of Him, or whether he will cut the cord.

Don't allow the baby God gives you to sever your relationship with Him. He allowed Abraham to raise Isaac, but He couldn't allow him to worship Isaac. There is another role that God will allow you to play in your baby's life. We can see an example of it in Luke, when Mary and Joseph are searching for Jesus, who at this point is twelve years old. Mary and Joseph have returned to Jerusalem for the Passover, and when it is time to leave, they notice that Jesus is not with them. They begin to look for Him and finally find Him sitting down, talking to doctors:

And he said unto them, how is it that ye sought me? Wist ye not that I must be about my father's business?

Luke 2:49 (King James Bible)

It is normal for a mother to be concerned about her child and to want to know his whereabouts. In this case, when Mary and Joseph express their concern about His absence, Jesus responds, "I must be about my father's business." What He is actually saying is, "You eventually will have to cut the cord. God allowed you the opportunity to get me here, but now I must do His will." Mary and Joseph soon find out that their roles have changed.

I know you carried that baby around for nine months and it's not easy to cut the cord, but you must if you want to move on to your next role in your child's life.

CONCLUSION

You now have discovered God's purpose for your life, but remember: cutting the cord does not end your responsibility. Your role has simply changed. You were carrying the child; now you're raising the child. You have moved from seeking your purpose to fulfilling it. Instead of needing someone to minister to you, you now should look for opportunities to minister to someone else.

You've completed your spiritual pregnancy, but life doesn't end when you find your purpose. Actually, you have found the real reason to live. God has created you to help someone. No one on this earth is like you; you're a designer's original, with specific gifts and talents that will allow you to minister to the people you are called to help. Remember, there are people waiting on you, looking for you, and depending on you to become all He made you to be.

Life takes on a whole new meaning when you discover your reason for being here. Now you understand that all the things you've experienced up to this point prepared you to solve someone else's problems. You have been given a ministry from God, who has equipped you to serve. He impregnated you with His plans for your life; you are now ready to live. I encourage you to keep learning, praying, and becoming more and more like Jesus.

I would love to hear how this book has blessed you. Please feel free to email @ kwa@kwaministries.org or write me @ P.O. Box 1295 Marrero, La. 70073

www.kwaministries.org

www.ingramcontent.com/pod-product-compliance
Lightning Source LLC
Chambersburg PA
CBHW071538040426
42452CB00008B/1063